The Four Steps to Healing

Catholic

2nd Edition

Martha Shuping, M.D.

Debbie McDaniel, M.A. LPC

Tabor Garden Press

2

Acknowledgments

Over the years, countless women have shared with us the stories of their abortions and miscarriages. This book is dedicated to them. Some of these women have chosen to reveal their stories privately, while others have come forward to speak out to the world. Through "Silent No More" programs, many women have been freed to tell their stories in public. Retreat experiences such as Rachel's Vineyard™ have encouraged women to share their experiences privately with other participants and to break the barriers of silence by talking to those they trust. As women are freed from feelings of guilt, they often become more comfortable sharing their experiences openly.

The stories that we have used in this book are based on real life situations that have been recounted to us. They do not represent individual case studies, but are rather composites of actual experiences. It is our desire that each woman will tell her own story in the way that will be the most freeing for her. Through the illustrations that we have included, we hope that women who have suffered in silence will recognize their own struggles and feel less isolated.

Through Rachel Network, an outreach formed to promote post-abortion healing, it is our intent to encourage support for those who are suffering from grief and loss, so that no woman will feel she has to carry her burden alone.

Martha Shuping, M.D.
and
Debbie McDaniel, M.A. LPC

Table of Contents

Introduction

Through my years of practice as a medical doctor in psychiatry and in the ministry of healing, I have had many professional and pastoral influences: I have learned from other medical doctors, from researchers, and also from clergy and lay ministers. Yet, I have been educated by my patients as well. In my work with countless women suffering from pregnancy loss, I have searched for ways to bring practical application to the theories I have learned. In studying both the mental health and pastoral literature, my goal has always been to discover what really works: for *real* people in *real* life.

One of my earliest influences was Sister Paula Vandegaer. While still in my psychiatry residency, after graduating from Wake Forest School of Medicine, I heard her speak in 1987 and learned of her four-step outline for healing. Her suggestions were both practical and profound. She emphasized the need for reconnecting with *others,* with the *child* who had been lost, with *God* and with *one's self* after experiencing the isolating pain of traumatic pregnancy loss. All four of these relationships must be gently restored in order for healing to take place.

The need for this restoration – indeed the *possibility* of such an experience – has been the foundation of post-abortion healing as it has developed over the years. In 1987, Kenneth McAll, M.D. and William P. Wilson, M.D. published an article on this subject in the *Southern Medical Journal.* They found that post-abortive patients who suffered with a variety of psychiatric symptoms (from depression to anorexia) experienced relief once they were given the opportunity to grieve their loss and then *reconnect* in some way: by praying for their child or offering a memorial service.

For many years, the rituals of mourning, traditionally offered to victims of bereavement, had been *denied* to women suffering the grief of pregnancy loss. But as the knowledge of this need began to evolve, so did those opportunities for commemorative healing that would finally lead to reconciliation with God, with the self and with the child.

It was out of this growing awareness that I developed the *Rachel Network Evening of Prayer for Healing After Abortion* in the early 1990's. This structured service created a practical application for the four areas highlighted by Sister Paula, and in keeping with the need for "ritual mourning" described by Drs. Wilson and McAll in 1987. Through prayer, music and meditation, in the spiritual setting of a candlelit chapel, the *Evening of Prayer* allowed women to acknowledge their grief – often for the first time. Yet, it also allowed them to experience the reality of their children enveloped in the presence of God. By naming their little ones and envisioning them in their own arms *and* in the arms of Jesus, many women were able to move beyond the guilt, fear and isolation that had held them captive.

The services were not limited to women who'd had abortions but were open to *all* who had been affected by this trauma in some way. By 1994, I was offering the *Rachel Network Evening of Prayer* regularly with clergy participation. A letter from a woman, several months after she had attended a service, describes her experience:

> *Because of your efforts in the Post-Abortion Services ... I have been able to move forward from years of guilt and low self-*

esteem; and now I'm finally feeling good about myself, because I can have a relationship with God.... I still visualize the things you suggested – I don't want to forget the true feeling of peace, forgiveness and love that I felt following that evening.

Over the course of many years of healing services and healing sessions, I have found that the *healing of the self* is ongoing. It is the final step of restoration that flows out of the reconnection with God's acceptance and love. This book is dedicated to those who seek that reconciliation and healing. It is for those who are hurting and for those who want to offer support as ministers, as professionals and as friends.

Martha Shuping, M.D.

How to Use This Book:
(Note to Professionals and those in Ministry)

In utilizing these materials, it is important to note that the four steps should not be thought of as a linear progression in which one phase follows the next in strict order. In some ways, these steps might be thought of as the four *bonds* of healing: four *relationships* that must be healed before restoration can take place. For some women, connecting with others by joining a group may help in connecting with God again. In other cases, an experience of the presence of God may help to break down the walls of isolation from others. The need to reconnect on all four levels is ever-present, and the healing in each of these relationships can occur at any time. Regardless of how that healing occurs, however, it is important that all four areas be addressed.

Over the years, I have studied many different models of healing. In most cases, I have found that a strictly medical model simply isn't enough. In psychiatry, even in instances where there are serious health concerns for the patient, a family systems model is usually needed to address issues with the primary support group, and a social work model is often needed to help access community resources. I have also seen the importance of pastoral models in addition to clinical ones. Patients in hospital settings often request visits from clergy and report benefit from prayer and spiritual support. And in the post-abortion recovery movement, women also testify to the benefits of the spiritual approach. Medical science cannot speak to the longings of women who wish to know that their children are in Heaven. And medical science cannot assure those who are struggling with guilt that they have been forgiven by a God who loves them. It is only by faith that these wounds can be healed and the relationships re-established.

While some clinicians might be uncomfortable with any discussion of spiritual dilemmas, the issues are very much on the minds of *many* women seeking post-abortion healing. In Rachel's Vineyard™, therapists and other healthcare professionals work together with those in ministry, using a model that incorporates psychological and spiritual issues within a pastoral framework. Therapists who feel the need to separate the spiritual from the emotional may want to make *referrals* rather than deal with post-abortion issues themselves. On the other hand, clinicians who *are* comfortable with the idea of incorporating a pastoral perspective may want to be involved in post-abortion recovery.

The pastoral post-abortion healing model is *proactive*. Therapists who are accustomed to sitting back and listening passively may want to try a more action-oriented approach than they would ordinarily use. Certainly, women who have been traumatized by abortion need to be *listened to* and *affirmed*. But they may also be at a loss when it comes to the steps necessary for their healing. Because of the secrecy surrounding abortion, the normal support systems for problem-solving are often inadequate or non-existent. While women may be inundated with advice on how to handle divorce, weight loss or other problems, they are unlikely to find day-time talk shows or mainstream magazines that tell them how to cope with their abortion. Additionally, women who would normally turn to their family or friends with their problems may not feel that they can come to them with grief over the termination of their pregnancy.

It is with these concerns in mind that this book has been written. It contains numerous practical ideas to make post-abortion recovery a *reality*. As you read through the pages of *The Four Steps to Healing*, you will notice distinct sections. There are individual illustrations – stories filled with many of the common experiences of those who have had been affected by abortion. These illustrations may help you to understand more deeply some of the issues faced by those who have suffered from post-abortion trauma. Though each person's experience will be unique, it is our hope that the stories we have included will provide an opportunity to reflect and to gain insight about the emotional and social conflicts of those you may be called to help in your work or ministry.

There are also Scriptural References, Prayers and Practical Suggestions located at the end of each chapter. It is our hope that *The Four Steps to Healing* will be a convenient reference tool for all who are involved in post-abortion recovery.

Martha Shuping, M.D.

Chapter One:
Reconnecting with Others

Healing can happen in many ways, but it's easier when you know you're not alone. Confronting the barriers of isolation that so often surround trauma is an important step. Most adults value their privacy, but it can be a curse rather than a blessing when it keeps people alienated from one another in their pain.

Prior to having an abortion, many women are told that it's "no big deal," "like having a tooth pulled." And yet, abortion is like nothing else. Dental extractions do not become family secrets. In fact, some surgeries are *family events*. Tonsillectomies and appendectomies are occasions for visits with flowers and cards as gestures of support for the recovering patient. But abortion is different: *no one is supposed to know*, and so the woman undergoing the procedure is denied the support that she needs.

However, as isolating as the experience can be, the decision to abort is not made in a vacuum. There are usually others involved in the choice. Pressures from parents and boyfriends can have a powerful impact. In recognition of this reality, the *Rachel Network Evening of Prayer*, from the beginning, has been offered to *all* who have been affected by abortion – both men and women. Though others may want to distance themselves from the pain, it is important for everyone involved to seek restoration. Too often, it has been the women alone who have carried the guilt and sought healing. At one of our first services, a crowd of men stood outside the church smoking cigarettes while their wives and girlfriends lined up inside for confession. Some of these men may have been the same ones who drove them to the abortion clinics in the first place. Perhaps they waited outside for them *there,* smoking cigarettes, trying to distance themselves from the pain of the experience. This gulf of separation is particularly painful for any woman whose sole confidante is her partner. When there is secrecy surrounding the pregnancy, a woman's boyfriend or husband may be the only one who knows. The abortion can become a painful wedge in a relationship that should be a source of mutual support.

Thankfully, over the years, more men have come forward to receive post-abortion healing. However, this is just one type of isolation that needs to be overcome when a traumatic pregnancy loss has occurred.

One of the most powerful aspects of the *Rachel Network Evening of Prayer* is that it gives people a chance to break down those walls of loneliness by coming together and joining in prayer with others. There is the opportunity to talk about the abortion (and the events that led up to it) in the Sacrament of Reconciliation. For some, this may be the first time they have ever discussed their experience with anyone. In the protected atmosphere of the confessional, women and men can retain their privacy while still having a human encounter that allows them to reconnect with the community and with God. Once this initial reconciliation has taken place, women may feel freer to evaluate *all* their relationships in a healing light. The following stories illustrate the effect that abortion can have on relationships.

Katherine was estranged from her mother for several years. Their relationship had never been the same after the abortion. Katherine had become pregnant as a teenager. She was scared and didn't know where to turn but finally decided to confide in her mom. She expected her disapproval since her mother was very religious and didn't believe in pre-marital sex. When she finally told her the truth, however, her mother seemed calm. She told Katherine that she would take her to see her Ob/Gyn. Katherine was nervous – she had never been to a gynecologist, before. But she felt relieved, believing that she and her baby were going to get the medical care they needed. She trusted her mother – *and* her mother's doctor. After all, this was the man who had brought her into the world.

Katherine's mother called his office to make the appointment. But what Katherine didn't realize was that the appointment wasn't for an examination – it was for an abortion.

Katherine had no idea what to expect, and she didn't know what was happening as she lay there on the table. The pain was excruciating, but it wasn't until after it was all over that she realized her baby was gone.

The loss seemed unreal at first. She knew that her mother didn't believe in abortion, and it seemed impossible that she would have arranged for her to have one. She tried to talk to her about it, but all her mom would say was that it was "for the best."

Katherine didn't make a conscious decision to hide her feelings, but it soon became a habit. She suppressed the anger, because she believed that her mother had only been trying to help. And she ignored other feelings that were too painful to face. After such a total loss of control on the table at the doctor's office, she developed a fear of losing control again. At the same time, she knew that she couldn't control everything. She avoided decisions but felt overwhelmed when anyone tried to decide *for her*.

By the time Katherine turned 18, she was eager to get out of the house, get married and start a family of her own. Once she did, however, she found herself on an emotional roller coaster. She would hide her feelings from her husband, Ned, giving him the impression that she was satisfied with his choices – at first. But over time, her frustrations surfaced and then began to explode. Ned insisted that they wait before starting a family. Katherine agreed but became resentful. As her real feelings aired, Ned became more reluctant to have children and wanted to wait *even longer*.

When they finally tried to conceive, Katherine had difficulty becoming pregnant. Her anger towards Ned became more volatile as she began to fear that she had wasted her fertile years waiting for him to be "ready." Yet, she also realized that her feelings were not aimed at him alone: she was still angry with her mother, too.

Katherine decided that in order to heal her relationship with her husband she needed to confront her feelings towards her mom. They had gone for a long time without even speaking. She wasn't sure how her mother would react, but she felt that her response didn't really matter as much as it had when she was seventeen. Her mother couldn't throw her out of her home or refuse to pay for her college tuition. There was no longer anything to dread, except the unpleasant feelings that they had been avoiding while avoiding each other. She decided to call her and tell her that she was angry about what she had done so many years before.

Her mother was surprised to hear from her after such a lapse of time and was distraught as she encountered

Katherine's anger. But she no longer tried to tell Katherine that the decision she imposed on her was "for the best." She, too, had regrets about the loss of the baby who would have been her first grandchild. Katherine's anger surprised her, but she had been angry with herself for years, and it was a relief to finally confront it – and to tell Katherine that she was sorry. After they had cried together, Katherine was surprised at how easy it was to forgive her mother for what she had done. She had needed her mother's acknowledgment that something was wrong. The forgiveness that her mother asked for validated the feelings she had kept hidden.

Once Katherine forgave her mother, her anger towards her husband no longer seemed so overwhelming. It was easier to be honest with him about her feelings. When she finally did conceive, she was better able to bond with her baby, since the rupture in her relationship with her own mother had been healed. And, as her relationship with her husband became more honest, she found it easier to be a parent with him and to be the mother that she had always wanted to be.

Greg didn't feel that he was ready to be a father when his girlfriend got pregnant. He didn't tell Sarah what to do, but he didn't offer any support, either. When Sarah had the abortion, he told himself that it was "her choice," and although she seemed angry about it, he convinced himself that she would feel better after it was over. For years, however, Sarah stayed angry. Sometimes her anger was quiet and unspoken; at other times she lashed out. She never mentioned the abortion, but Greg often wondered if that was on her mind when she yelled at him for "not being there" for her. Greg tried to appease her because he didn't like conflict. He sometimes thought they would be better off apart, but he was afraid of being alone. Finally, she gave him an ultimatum: she was leaving unless he agreed to get married.

Greg felt cornered – just as he had when she found out she was pregnant. He didn't really want to lose Sarah, but he still didn't feel ready for marriage and a family. Greg sought advice from his friends. Some of them didn't like Sarah, but they all agreed she was right: it was time for Greg to break up with her or get married and get on with his life.

Only one friend knew the whole story, however. Andy had known Greg since high school. When Greg found out Sarah was pregnant, Andy had told them where to go to get the abortion. That's because Andy and his fiancée, Grace, had done the same thing before they got married. Years later, Grace regretted her abortion and became depressed. Grace began searching online to find help and had come across a program called Rachel's Vineyard™. She and Andy had participated in one of their retreats, and it had changed their lives. Andy realized that his unresolved feelings about the abortion had made him ambivalent about their relationship. He wondered if the same thing might be happening to Greg.

Greg wanted to talk to Sarah about it, but he didn't know how. He realized that Sarah had never been the same since they decided to have an abortion. He wondered if they could ever be as happy as they were before. He went online to look at the Rachel's Vineyard™ website and decided to leave it on the screen so that Sarah would find it.

At first, she was furious when she saw it. She felt that Greg had no business reading about other women's abortions. But Greg said that he needed help, too. He pointed out that the retreats were open to men, as well as women, and he wanted to go.

Sarah wasn't interested at first. She told Greg that he could go alone if he wanted to, but she didn't believe he would really do it. Greg surprised her by registering for the retreat that same day. When she saw that he was determined to go, she decided to go with him.

Although she had no expectations of healing, she used the opportunity to vent her anger and finally revealed to Greg how betrayed she'd felt by the way he had responded to her pregnancy. Greg admitted that he was angry at himself for not being stronger. When they got past the anger, there were other feelings to be explored: feelings of grief, loss and vulnerability. Sharing their underlying emotions brought them closer together. By the end of the weekend, they both felt that a weight had been lifted. Neither of them was sure if marriage was the right course for them, but they decided to try pre-marital counseling to explore their future together.

Gail was happy when she found out she was pregnant at seventeen. Of course, she had originally planned to get married first – after her fiancée finished his military training – but the timing wasn't all that important to her. She knew that they would be married in a few months, and she was excited about being a mother for the first time.

Her family, however, felt differently. They were embarrassed at the idea of their daughter being pregnant outside of wedlock. They were prominent in the community and concerned about their reputation. Her mother told her that if she wanted to continue to live at home, she would have to have an abortion. Gail knew that

17

her mother wasn't really offering her a choice: she didn't give her permission to live elsewhere or try to help her find another home. She wanted her daughter to terminate the pregnancy.

Gail tried desperately to find alternative housing. Her husband-to-be was temporarily out of reach because of his military assignment. So, Gail was really on her own for a few crucial weeks. Since she was still a minor, there were legal complications that prevented her from taking advantage of the shelter homes that were available to women over eighteen.

Her mom didn't give her much time: when Gail's attempts to get away from home failed, she drove her to the abortion clinic. Gail thought that she would still have a chance to save her baby, however. She couldn't believe that they would do the procedure without her permission. She let the staff at the clinic know her decision in no uncertain terms: "I don't give my consent for this," she said. She was shocked by their response, however. One nurse told her to "grow up." When Gail tried to get up and leave, she was restrained and then sedated.

Gail's relationship with her mother had never been good, but after that, it got worse. Over the years, Gail's anger towards her *grew* – and towards the staff at the clinic who ignored her wishes. She also struggled with feelings of depression and anxiety because of the trauma she had endured. Yet, Gail did find healing. Eventually, for her own peace of mind, she decided to forgive her mother and to maintain some contact with her. However, she has had to learn to set boundaries to protect herself from the kind of personal violation she suffered in the past.

Rianna has forgiven everyone who has hurt her, but she hasn't let them all remain in her life. She became pregnant after being raped. *For her*, forgiveness meant letting go and letting God deal with her attacker and with the other people who had wounded her without any remorse. It took her many years to get to that point, but she finally realized that she was hurting *herself* by holding on to the rage. She needed to express her anger and have it validated by her therapist. But in the end, she realized that staying stuck in those emotions gave too much power to those who had violated her. By forgiving them, she allowed herself to be free from everything that tied her to those people.

The stories of *Katherine, Greg, Gail* and *Rianna,* show very different approaches to reconnecting with others. Sometimes people believe that forgiveness means reconciliation. But, as illustrated by the examples above, forgiveness can have a variety of outcomes. Jesus forgave the people who crucified him, but his relationships with them varied according to their responses to *him*. As he died on the Cross, two men expired beside him, but only *one* of them received this promise: "I tell you, this day, you will be with me in Paradise." The man who had cruelly mocked Jesus in his moment of agony missed out on the reconciliation that the other man experienced when he expressed remorse and a desire to connect: "Remember me, when you come into your Kingdom." (Lk. 23:42-43)

Jesus responded openly to those who really wanted to be with him – and to all those who were honest about what they needed and desired from him. But he didn't compromise himself for those whose only goal was to hurt him. His prayer on the cross shows that he forgave even those who *refused his love* – proving that it is possible to forgive those who don't say, "I'm sorry." We can be at peace even when others refuse to make peace with us.

Not every story of forgiveness ends up the way that Katherine's did, with her mother expressing guilt, and the two of them coming to a deeper understanding. There may be people in your life who will never understand what they did or show regret for their actions. In some cases, you may still need to take legal action against them, even press criminal charges if warranted. However, that doesn't mean that you are required to carry the burden of resentment all your life.

Sometimes confrontation can be healing – in other cases, it may be too dangerous. You might need to consult a professional to help you decide whether it's safe or not to have a relationship with someone who has hurt you in the past. Talking to a therapist, a pastor, a police officer or an attorney (depending on the situation) may help to clarify the appropriate course of action.

And yet, even in cases where you can't speak to the person who has wronged you, there *are* ways that you can let your anger out. Prayer can be an empowering tool for forgiveness. You might want to picture Jesus' hands in front of you and place all the people who have hurt you in his palms. Writing a letter to vent your feelings can also be healing. *Sending* the letter isn't necessary. In fact, once you've written down your feelings, you may find it more satisfying to burn or shred the pages to give yourself a sense of closure. Having an imaginary conversation can also give you a chance to say what you want and not have to worry about how the other person will respond.

Forgiveness is an acknowledgement that God is bigger than the people who have injured us. As we free ourselves from the hold that they have over our lives, we can make room for healthy relationships with people who are supportive and caring.

The *Rachel Network Evening of Prayer for Healing After Abortion* is a good first step for reconnecting. But support groups and weekend retreats such as Rachel's Vineyard™ can also be powerful – along with professional counseling and psychotherapy. Having others around you for support and validation is conducive to healthy emotional processing.

God is a great defender of those who have been oppressed and abused. In Scripture, we can find countless examples of Him defending the downtrodden and the oppressed. The story of Joseph, in the Book of Genesis, is a great example of how God works in the lives of those who choose to move beyond the pain of the past. Joseph was sold into slavery by his own brothers, but was freed from prison in Egypt and then elevated to the highest rank next to Pharaoh. God protected Joseph in all his struggles.

Joseph, for his part, was willing to forgive his brothers. And yet, when they finally came to him, he needed time to work through his feelings. He didn't express his forgiveness right away. He let his brothers experience some of the same anxiety that he had endured himself. He allowed them to be falsely accused, and to feel the fear that they might be imprisoned. But in the end Joseph let them know that he saw God's hand in the situation and that *their* intentions didn't matter to him as much as *God's*. God vindicated Joseph, and Joseph knew that he had nothing to gain by holding on to the hurts of the past.

The story of David's life is also a good example of the power of forgiveness. When David was betrayed, he counted on God to be his defender. In the Psalms, David freely expresses anger and hurt through his songs. But he also conveys forgiveness and confidence in God's love and support.

David's willingness to forgive others helped him to experience forgiveness, himself, when he was riddled with guilt after making a bad choice. David had become involved in a relationship that he should never have sought in the first place. He ended up having an unplanned pregnancy with a married woman named Bathsheba. When their child was seriously ill at birth, David was stricken with grief, as well as guilt. But by praying for his son, and by helping Bathsheba with her grief after the child died, David was able to begin the process of healing for himself as well.

Scripture for Meditation:

"Hear, O Lord, my plea for justice: pay heed to my cry. Listen to my prayer spoken in truth. From You, let my vindication come. Your eyes see what is right." (Psalm 17:1-2)

"I call upon you – answer me, O God -- turn Your ear towards me and hear my prayer. Show me Your wonderful love. With Your right arm, You deliver those who seek refuge from their foes. Keep me as the apple of Your eye. Hide me in the shadow of Your wings from the violence of the wicked." (Psalm 17:6-9)

"Behold how good and pleasant it is, when brethren dwell together …. It is a dew like that of Hermon which comes down upon the mountain of Zion: for, there, the Lord has pronounced His blessing forever." (Psalm 133)

Prayer:

Lord, we thank You for helping us to break down the barriers that have kept us from connecting with others in a healthy way. Free us from destructive relationships and release us from the resentment and bitterness that keep us stuck in old patterns. Only Your love and healing can bring freedom of forgiveness. We place in Your hands the people who have wounded us so deeply. May their power to hurt us diminish as we make room for Your grace by letting go. Surround us with Your Spirit. Protect us from those who have injured us in the past and allow us to form newer, stronger relationships based on Your infinite love and mercy.

Lord, You intended the bonds of family and friendship to be a blessing forever – anointed by Your Love. Let us be truly blessed in those we care about. If we have attachments to people who are destructive and abusive, we ask you to free us and provide us with new relationships in Your extended family.

Let Your healing flow like fresh, life-giving springs into our churches, our communities, into our homes, and into the bonds of each special friendship. May Your light shine through us, as we become a light to the people around us.

Amen.

Review of Practical Suggestions:

1. Write a Letter to Express Feelings. Women who felt abandoned or rejected during their pregnancy may have particular anger towards those who weren't there for them when they most needed their help. In *Aborted Women Silent No More* (1987), researcher David Reardon published the results of a study of women seeking help after an abortion in which seventy-three percent indicated that they felt "forced" into that course of action by someone else, *at least to some degree.* Eighty-four percent said that they felt forced by *circumstances* and eighty-eight percent felt that they might have chosen differently with some encouragement. These figures indicate that there are many women who did not get the support they needed from those closest to them. Identifying the people who let us down, and expressing anger towards them in a healthy way, can be an important step in the healing process.

Writing a letter may be preferable to saying things face to face. Whether you want to express anger or forgiveness, a letter can be a useful tool. However, if your only intention is to vent your feelings, it's important not to send a letter that could be construed as *threatening.* And be cautious about writing a letter to someone whom you don't want to see again. A letter that includes a lot of *"Why-did-you-do-that?"* questions may be construed as an invitation for further contact. If your intention is to forgive, remember that forgiveness is not the same thing as reconciliation. Letting go of past hurts doesn't necessarily mean letting someone back in your life.

Taking the step to *send* an expressive letter is something that should be carefully evaluated. Seek the

24

counsel of someone objective – such as a therapist or a pastor. In cases of divorce or abuse, or in any case where there may be legal ramifications, consult an *attorney* for advice as well. A letter doesn't have to be sent to be powerful. It can simply be a way to purge negative feelings and find validation by committing them to paper.

There are many factors to consider. For pure emotional release, writing a letter *without* having to worry about the consequences of sending it can be very freeing. You might want to write two letters: first, an uncensored version (to get things off your chest and then to *shred* afterwards) and second, an edited version that will address whatever goal you wish to accomplish in your relationship with the other person – whether that might be *ending* the relationship or *improving* it.

2. Join a Group. A mentioned before, Rachel's Vineyard Retreat™ provides secure group settings during its weekend format and can be a good first step for re-establishing trust in others.

Therapy and support groups can provide a safe way to connect and break down barriers of isolation. Therapists may want to direct their post-abortive clients into an appropriate group setting. The abortion itself is often not the only issue. Groups that deal with sexual abuse, eating disorders, or substance abuse may be beneficial. Self-esteem issues may also need to be addressed. If a referral to a therapy group is made, it is important to make sure that the leaders will be sensitive to post-abortion issues.

In the Garden of the New Creation (from Tabor Garden Press) is a spiritual self-esteem workbook that has been used in post-abortion recovery. It deals with a variety of issues including mental health concerns (such as depression and anxiety) and personal growth skills (boundary-setting and decision-making, for example). These are important components of the healing process. This book is often used in a group format where women come together to encourage each other in their healing.

There are many types of group experiences available. Pregnancy care centers sometimes offer support groups for those who have experienced miscarriages or abortion. They can also provide referrals to therapists and recommendations about community resources. Contact your Diocesan Respect Life or Project Rachel Office to find out more about what's being offered in your area.

3. Tell a Trusted Friend or Family Member. The Rachel's Vineyard Retreat™ provides a built-in opportunity to include close family and friends in the healing process. It allows them to share the grief just as they would if a child were lost under any other circumstances. The Memorial Service at the end of the weekend is open to anyone whom participants wish to invite, and a support person can also be brought along for the entire weekend if desired. Developing a support system of people who know about the loss and care enough to help is crucial to the healing process.

4. Get Involved. A traumatic abortion can affect every aspect of a woman's life. For those who have withdrawn from social activities because of fear, guilt or depression, participating in activities once again can be revitalizing. Churches are often great places to get involved and make friends. They can also provide surrogate families when primary relationships have been broken. However, something as simple as joining a bowling team or a health club can be therapeutic too.

5. Do a Boundary Check. Being over-involved can be as much of a problem as being under-involved. After a pregnancy loss, some people fill the void with *too many* activities – and with demanding, unhealthy relationships. Re-evaluate commitments to make sure that you have time and space to heal.

6. Make a Difference. Once women have experienced some healing through *safe* sharing experiences, they may feel ready to broaden their horizons. One way of reaching out is sharing information. For some women, working in a crisis pregnancy center can be healing. Helping others who are struggling and vulnerable can be a way to heal recollections from the past. By giving appropriate support, the painful memory of *needing* support can be transformed.

Additionally, as mentioned earlier, many women have experienced validation and relief through *Silent No More* programs where those who have undergone abortions have come forward to tell their stories publicly. Some have lobbied congress for better *informed consent* laws. Others, who wish to testify that they have been harmed by the abortion industry, have taken legal action. Not everyone feels comfortable with steps such as these, but many women do consider it cathartic to come forth after being silenced by society. Each woman must determine her point of readiness without being pressured. In any case, changing the world for the better, in some way, can be a great antidote for feelings of helplessness and loss of control.

7. **Forgive.** Forgiveness is the ongoing process that underlies our ability to reconnect with others in healthy ways. Below, are some steps that can be taken towards inner peace and freedom. If you still feel stuck, you may want to work through some of your issues with *In the Garden of the New Creation,* which contains exercises for those who are struggling to find closure through forgiveness.

(**A.**) *Acknowledge the hurt.* We can't *forgive* until we acknowledge that we have been wounded. Exploring *all* our feelings, including anger, sadness and fear, is necessary to allow healing to happen.

(**B.**) *Bring it to God.* God can heal our scars and restore the dignity that is lost when we are aggrieved, abandoned or attacked. Making God our confidante can help relieve the sting of *trust violated* by others and *promises broken.* Tell God about the person who has hurt you. Even if you are angry as you pray, the act of bringing those who have wounded you to the Lord will help you to begin the healing process.

(**C.**) *Choose to be free.* There are many things that we can't control. Our lives are affected by the actions that others take and the choices they make. We can't choose our enemies and we can't always choose our friends. We can't choose our family members or the people who go to our church, and we can't necessarily choose how we feel about them, *either.* But we can choose to give our feelings to God. We can choose to give Him our relationships (both the ones that we want to *continue* and the ones that we need to *end.*) And we can choose to lay our burdens down before the Lord rather than carry them inside of us. God may not change our feelings or our friendships right away, but over time, if we continue to make a conscious choice to be free of bitterness and resentment, He can transform the things that we can't change on our own.

(**D.**) *Decide on a course of action.* It's almost always easier to change our behavior than to change the way that we feel. In fact, our feelings may be the *last* thing to change when we forgive. Choose a course of action that makes forgiveness real. Plan something that you can do (with God's help) over the course of several months. Forgiveness is not a one-time event but an ongoing process. One woman found healing by preparing a manger for Christ over the course of a year. Every time someone hurt her, she offered it to the Lord and placed a piece of straw in a basket. By Christmastime she had a soft, warm bed, lovingly filled with acts of mercy to welcome the Child Jesus. Think about what would work for you. Make a commitment to pray each night for those who have offended you. If you don't know what to say, try this simple prayer: "Jesus, I ask you to help me to forgive _____. Let me draw on the mercy that flows from your Cross." If you tend to be a visual person, picture yourself bringing those who have hurt you to the Lord. Or find a Scripture verse that you can repeat when you are tempted by bitter thoughts. Sometimes forgiveness is simply a matter to be addressed with God. This is especially true in cases where the people who hurt us are not safe to be around. In other cases, however, we may want to reach out and let others know how we feel. A misunderstanding with a friend can often be resolved with a simple phone call. But if there has been a longstanding estrangement, you may need to take some time to consider the best way to reconnect. If you're not sure how the other person will react, but are certain that you want to re-establish contact, a brief e-mail might be the best way to open the lines of communication. Asking a friend to dinner is a thoughtful way to make peace after an argument, and a warm meal can alleviate awkward silences.

(E.) *Establish boundaries.* Pray about the kind of relationship that you want to have with the person who has hurt you. In some cases, you may want to forgive *without having any contact.* If the person is violent, a restraining order or legal charges may be necessary. In other cases, you may wish to forgive and reconcile but have only *limited contact.* On the other hand, there are probably other relationships that you hope to deepen. In those cases, you will still need boundaries, but you will want them to be wide enough to allow for communication and caring. Pray about the parameters that you want to establish, and then take appropriate steps. If you've had difficulty setting boundaries in the past, get support and feedback from someone impartial.

(F.) *Focus on God.* If we think only about the hurts that we have endured, and become discouraged by our limited ability to forget, we may find it impossible to forgive. But God is bigger than our limitations. If we keep our eyes on Him and remember the forgiveness that He has offered to us, we will find the strength that we need to offer that forgiveness to others.

(G.) *Give thanks.* Recognizing the *good* that God is able to bring out of our sufferings can give us a sense of our struggles being "worth it." Remember Joseph, whose brothers sold him into slavery in Egypt. When he contemplated the way that God used his experiences to raise him up and rescue the world from famine, it made it easier for him to forgive. And when King David, as a boy, had been left to ward off lions and bears from the family flocks with nothing but a slingshot, *he bore no ill will towards his brothers who left him alone in the fields*. David saw God's hand in his circumstances and was able to thank Him for the way He had prepared him for great victories later in life. Jesus also glorified God when He contemplated the Cross. He focused on the victory of his death, knowing that his sufferings would be vindicated in the Resurrection. *Gratitude* is one of the secret keys to forgiveness that can actually change the way we feel. There is *real joy* in seeing how God works in our lives when we let go and let His Grace flow freely.

(**H.**) *Hope for Healing.* When we are hurting, it's natural to want to strike out at the person who has inflicted our pain. Yet, oftentimes, our *real* desire is simply for the other person to *feel what we are feeling.* If they frightened us in the past, we may want them to be filled with fear. If they berated us, we may want them to feel shame. This isn't necessarily a desire for retaliation – shared feelings promote empathy and emotional understanding. There's nothing wrong with wanting others to feel our pain and to understand the impact of their own hurtful actions. Yet, *their* awareness of wrongdoing may be blocked by hurts of their own. They may have been wounded in the same way that they wounded us. All our powers of persuasion may not be enough to change another person's perspective or induce them to say, "I'm sorry." But God *can* bring about change. He so thoroughly understands the hearts He has made, that He is able to inspire repentance and restoration.

God can teach those who have hurt us to feel their own pain and *ours*. Through His grace, we can hope to find healing for ourselves and for the other person, as well.

Notes:

_____

_____

_____

_____

_____

_____

_____

_____

_____

_____

_____

Notes:

Notes:

Notes:

Notes:

Notes:

Notes:

Chapter Two:
Reconnecting with Your Child

In the Scriptures, King David prayed for his child, and this helped him to move on with his life as he confronted his sorrow. Accepting a child who's been lost as *a real person* may be difficult at first, but it is *this step* that truly validates the feelings of grief. When others tell us that "it wasn't a real baby yet," they may mean well, but statements like that trivialize the loss that is involved in abortion and miscarriage. One woman who'd had three abortions said, "They told me that having an abortion would be like an eraser – that it would make the pregnancy go away. But if it was an *eraser,* then how come I know how old my children would be today?" Acknowledging our children is a way of saying: "I'm not crazy for having these feelings. I lost something important."

As we discussed in the introduction, rituals and symbolic gestures may help with this part of the healing process. The emotion of grief when confronting the loss of a loved one can be overpowering. Events such as funerals and memorial services provide us with maps that can guide us through the passages of mourning.

Dealing with the death of an unborn child can present particular difficulties. When you are grieving a child whom you never had a chance to know, it can be even *more* difficult to put your feelings into words. Consider the following stories of grief and healing.

Maggie always wanted to be a mother. She imagined having a little girl to dress up and play with. She had never been close to her own mother, and she wanted a chance to relive her childhood with a daughter of her own. She anticipated buying the dolls that she had never gotten, going to the park and out shopping, and sharing all those experiences with someone who truly belonged to her. When she got pregnant before she graduated from college, her picture-perfect dream seemed impossible. Although she felt an immediate bond with the child she was carrying, she knew that it would be years before she would be in a position to give her the life that she wanted to share with her. Maggie didn't want to give up her child. In fact, she even decided on a name for her: *Madeline.* She loved her, but she just didn't want Madeline to show up quite so soon. Having an abortion seemed like a way to put her daughter on the shelf for a few years – until she was ready for her.

Maggie didn't mourn over Madeline right away. After the abortion, she threw herself into her studies, and then into her career. She was even more driven to succeed after the abortion. She was determined to make enough money to create the life that she wanted for herself and her child. As the years passed, however, her life grew more and more hectic. She never did find the perfect father for the perfect marriage that she wanted for her *one perfect child.* The real father of the baby that she had given up had been heart-broken when she ended their relationship, but he married someone else and had four little girls. All of them looked just the way Maggie had imagined her own daughter: with blond hair and green eyes.

When Maggie got married at last, she was in her thirties. This time, getting pregnant didn't come quite so easily. When she finally conceived, it was different from her expectations. Somehow, in her mind she had always imagined that getting pregnant would unite her with Madeline again – and that this time, nothing would come between them. However, when she suffered a miscarriage, that illusion was shattered. Her next pregnancy was difficult as well. As it progressed, she became more and more aware that the child she was carrying was not the one that she fantasized about for so many years. This time, she had a sense that her baby was a boy. The ultrasound confirmed her intuition, and as he grew inside of her, he showed signs of having a personality that would always be at odds with her own. Micah was a fighter. This trait served him well when he was born prematurely, but Maggie wondered if she would ever be the kind of mother that he needed. As he grew, he struggled with Maggie constantly. The days that she spent contending with his tantrums were a far cry from the blissful afternoons that she had that she had envisioned: strolling through the park with a peaceful, smiling baby.

It wasn't that she didn't love Micah. He meant more to her than her own life. After waiting so long to conceive again, and then enduring two difficult pregnancies, she knew that Micah's life was a miracle. Her previous expectations only made her feel guilty. She felt bad for wanting a girl. And she blamed herself for feeling so unprepared to meet the needs of her little boy.

Every time her feelings of grief began to surface, Maggie reproached herself. She told herself that it was ridiculous to mourn over a "fantasy" when she had "the real thing" with Micah. But her grief didn't go away. And neither did her desire to try again for a girl.

As time went by – and her hope of getting pregnant again diminished – the grief became harder to ignore. She began to realize that she was never going to be the mother that she wanted to be until she faced her feelings about the motherhood she had lost. Micah was real, but the child of her first pregnancy was real too. She might not have had green eyes or blond hair – but she was a real person, whom Maggie had loved and lost. The child of her miscarriage was real, too, though Maggie's feelings, at the time, had been absorbed by the urgency of her subsequent pregnancy with Micah.

Maggie began going to therapy to explore the grief that she had held in for so long. As she mourned her losses, she began to accept *all* of her children for *who they really were* – whether they lived up to her expectations or not. She wrote letters to express her feelings. She still had a sense that Madeline was a girl, just as she had sensed that Micah was a boy even before he was born. And as she thought about it, she had a hunch that her second child had been a boy too. She shared her feelings with her husband, John, who had never expressed his grief about the miscarriage before. At first, he had a hard time talking about the child they had lost – he wanted to focus on the present, and on Micah. But he knew that something needed to change – and, as he supported Maggie in her mourning, he recognized that he was grieving too. He had dreamed of having a big family with a house full of brothers and sisters for Micah.

Although he had never thought of the child they miscarried as a real person, John finally understood that they needed to recognize him in some way. Naming their lost child gave Maggie and John something *real* to help fill the empty places in their life. Maggie wrote a letter to *Marcus,* and John made a woodcarving to commemorate him.

42

Maggie also decided to tell John about the pregnancy that she had given up before she met him. She was afraid of how he would react, but she no longer wanted to carry her secret alone. He was surprised but supportive. It had never occurred to him that Maggie could still be feeling the effects of something that had happened so long ago. But he understood that Madeline was a part of his life too, because she was important to his wife.

In addition to therapy, Maggie and John had faith that helped them to confront their losses. Both of them felt convinced that Madeline and Marcus were in Heaven. As they imagined them there, in a place of peace and comfort, Maggie and John began to feel more at peace as well – with themselves, with God and with all their children. And when Maggie began to feel more comfortable with herself as a mother, her relationship with Micah began to improve.

Now Maggie, is able to *enjoy* being a mom. Although her feelings of grief didn't "just go away," she no longer feels guilty for having them. Recognizing her other children has helped her to feel more at ease with herself and more confident in her relationship with her son.

Betsy had told very few people about her abortion. However, when her daughter, Maribeth, turned four, she began to talk about her "sister." Betsy and her husband, Tom, tried to tell her that she was an "only child," but Maribeth kept insisting that she had a sister up in Heaven called "Baby." Betsy had never thought about the child she had lost until Maribeth brought it up. She tried not to take it too seriously, but she couldn't escape the feeling that their daughter had some mysterious connection with their first child. She felt unnerved by this reminder of the past.

Tom, however, was even more shaken. He felt haunted by the child he never knew.

Finally, they decided to give Baby a name of her own: *Angelica*. Instead of imagining her as a ghost who was oppressing their family, they wanted to see her as a little "angel" watching over them from Heaven. Once Angelica had a name, they no longer felt afraid of her.

They debated about what to tell Maribeth, but they found that she no longer asked about Baby once they had made their peace with her. Betsy and Tom decided that when Maribeth was older, they would tell her about her sister and about their experience with the abortion. They hope that by discussing their own experiences with her, she will be better prepared for life than they had been when they first began dating each other in high school.

Macey had gotten pregnant when she was just fifteen. She was terrified when she found out. All she wanted was to make it go away. When she went to the clinic, *that was exactly what they promised her.* They told her that it would be as if she had never even been pregnant at all.

Macey felt relieved when she made her decision. She imagined that she was going to turn back the calendar and start her month all over again. However, the procedure wasn't as easy as they had promised her. She had a great deal of pain and bleeding.

Afterward, she worried that maybe something was really wrong, and that she would never be able to have children at all. Suddenly, the pregnancy she had lost wasn't just a pregnancy ... *maybe it was the only child she would ever have.* She began to wonder about whether her baby had been a boy or a girl. She wished that she would get pregnant again to reassure herself that she could still conceive. Macey didn't make a conscious decision to try again, but she had so many fears about her fertility that her previous fear of getting pregnant seemed to fade into the background.

She stopped using birth control. It hadn't kept her from getting pregnant before, so it wasn't hard for her to convince herself that she didn't need it, now. And she was scared about what it might be doing to her body. Within a year, she was pregnant again. This time, she felt relieved. She was elated to know that she was still able to conceive.

Her boyfriend wasn't happy at all, however, and when the reality of the situation set in, so did the fear. Macey had another abortion since she didn't know what else to do. The next time Macey got pregnant, she started drinking to drive away her anxiety, but then she felt that she had to terminate the pregnancy out of fear that she might have harmed her child with alcohol.

She ended up having a total of five abortions. None of them ever "made it go away." When she graduated from college, she thought about how old her children would be. On every birthday and holiday, she wondered what it would have been like to share the experience with them.

Macey's children were a permanent fixture in her mind, and she grieved over the fact that they weren't a part of her life. Over the years, she felt as if she had watched them grow through a window that separated them from her. "Daisy" would have been fourteen – just starting high school. "Charlie" would have been thirteen. "Chelsea" would have been in the sixth grade. She thought about the books that she would have given them, and her childhood toys that they could have inherited. Maybe "Ashley" would have gotten her favorite doll, and "Chad" could have had her old tricycle.

When Macey attended a Rachel's Vineyard Retreat™, she wrote each of them a letter and told all of them about her wishes for them. She expressed how much she had missed knowing them as they grew up. For the first time, she felt as if she had opened the window to reach out to them.

After the retreat, she had a sense that she had regained something she had lost, and she was ready to let go of some of the things that she had been holding on to. She decided to give away the toys that she had been saving. She didn't want them to sit alone on their shelves any more. She had missed out on the joy of sharing her childhood treasures, and she wanted to have that experience at last.

After writing letters to her children in Heaven, she began to see how powerful it could be to connect with someone in that way. She decided to sponsor five needy children in other countries and to get to know them by writing letters. It was a big commitment, but she was ready to have obligations in her life and to respond to children who needed her.

Little by little, Macey found tangible ways to reconnect with her sons and daughters. And in doing so, she was able to find a whole new life of connecting with others. Now the window is always open, and she no longer feels that barrier of separation between herself and the rest of the world.

Nola believed that her children were in Heaven, but that didn't help her, initially. She was convinced that they hated her. In spite of her faith in God, she was sure that she could never go to Heaven and face the four children she had given up. Finally, when her fear and guilt became too much, she attended a *Rachel Network Evening of Prayer.* There, she had a chance to visualize each of her children with Jesus. In his loving eyes, she no longer felt condemned, and she had the courage to imagine her babies in *her* arms as well as *his*.

Afterwards, as Nola reflected on the children that she had pictured that night, she no longer felt afraid of their anger. Their faces seemed sweet and full of love. She began to feel a desire to be closer to them and wrote a letter to each of them asking them to forgive her. She was surprised at how freeing it felt. It no longer seemed as if they were looking down from Heaven and judging her. They seemed to be reaching out to her with tenderness, instead. Now, Nola no longer fears meeting them in Heaven. And she no longer fears being reminded of them here on earth. They are her children. Though she let go of them once, having been reconciled to them again through Christ, she has found a true, lasting love that no one can ever take away from her.

Brandy avoided babies. When she saw other people's children, she became angry and afraid. She didn't like to remember her abortion, and she didn't want to have any feelings for the child that she could have had. She avoided thinking about motherhood for years, swearing that she would never get pregnant again.

Eventually, however, she fell in love and got married. Her maternal desires began to emerge when her husband wanted to have a baby. At first, she was pleased when she became pregnant. It wasn't until her first ultrasound that her old fears returned. She also felt something new: *guilt*. When she saw the picture of the baby she was carrying and learned that it was a boy, she was struck with the realization that her first baby had been a real person, too, at that same early stage. Suddenly Brandy was terrified at the thought of progressing through her pregnancy. It seemed that each new phase would be a confirmation of what she had lost. In her fear, she contemplated having an abortion again, but she knew that her husband would be devastated. And deep down, she knew that she still wanted to have a family with the man she loved.

Brandy sought counseling to confront her fears. She realized that she needed to acknowledge her first child in order to bond with her second. She attended a Rachel's Vineyard Retreat™ where she began a relationship with both of her children. Freed from the fear and guilt of the past, she was able to enjoy watching the child inside of her grow and develop.

Trissa never got what she needed from her own mother. As a child, she was kept by relatives and baby-sitters who didn't really care about her. When she became pregnant herself, she didn't know how to give someone else the nurturing that she had never received. She longed for a close relationship with a child she could love, but it seemed impossible, so she decided to end the pregnancy. After the abortion, however, she was heartsick. She cried every night – for her baby and for herself.

When Trissa finally attended a *Rachel Network Evening of Prayer,* she not only pictured her baby in the arms of Jesus: she pictured *herself.* As she imagined being cradled in the strong arms of the Lord, she felt loved for the first time. Reconnecting with the baby she had lost allowed her to reconnect with *herself* as a child. As she nurtured

48

him, she began to nurture her own spirit. She realized that there was a part of her that was still crying out for love and affection.

Trissa's healing became a part of her bonding experience. Naming her baby helped to strengthen her own identity. And as she expressed her love for him in cards and letters, she began to love herself in a deeper way. When Trissa finally fell in love and got married, she wasn't just trying to fill a void. She was ready to share herself with someone else. And when she got pregnant, she had new resources to meet her baby's needs.

Trissa wasn't able to heal on her own. Her faith in God allowed her to draw on *His* love to fill her needs and the needs of her children. God had enough love for all of them, and through focused prayer, she was able to receive the care and nurturing that He had to offer.

In the Gospel of Life, John Paul II offers reassuring words to women who have known the grief and loss of abortion: "You will come to understand that nothing is definitively lost, and you will also be able to ask forgiveness from your child who is now living with the Lord." (Par. 99)

Reconnecting with the child who has been lost is integral to the healing process. But it can be a challenge as well. The loss can seem intangible, and the *person* inside the pregnancy can be hard to identify. Through the science surrounding fetal development, we know that the child was real. Through faith, we know that he or she is real, still. A belief in eternal life, with Christ at the center, allows us to connect with *all* who are alive in him. The following Scriptures and practical suggestions may help to re-establish that bond.

Scripture for Meditation:

"Before I formed you in the womb I knew you, before you were born, I sanctified you ...." (Jer. 1:5)

"Let the little children come to me – do not hinder them – the reign of God belongs to such as these." (Luke 18: 16)

"Fear not, for I have redeemed you, I have called you by name and you are Mine .... Fear not, I am with you: I will bring back your descendents from the East, and from the West, I will gather them to you. I will say to the North: 'Give them up!' and to the South: 'Don't hold back! Bring back My sons from afar and My daughters from the ends of the earth. Everyone named as Mine, whom I created for My glory, whom I formed and made.'" (Isaiah 43)

"For I am certain that neither death nor life, nor angels nor principalities, neither the present nor the future, nor powers, neither height, nor depth, nor any other creature will be able to separate us from the love of God that comes to us in Christ Jesus, our Lord." (Romans 8:38-39)

Prayer:

Lord, You have promised that not even death can separate us from the love that we have in You. Our lives are already joined with Yours in Heaven. If we live in Your love, we have passed from death to life. Strengthen our union with You, so that we may be more closely united to all those who are alive in You – including the children that we long for.

Through Your love for them, let our love be strengthened and healed. We entrust our children into Your arms, and ask that You give us a sense of the peace, joy and comfort that they have in Heaven with You.

Amen.

Review of Practical Suggestions:

Events like Rachel's Vineyard Retreat™ and *The Rachel Network Evening of Prayer* provide a reassuring structure for those first tentative steps toward the child who may seem out of reach. Through years of facilitating these programs, we have often been amazed at how clearly many women sense their children's identities. Often they seem to know their features, personality and gender. In those cases, the name has seemed just as obvious: "Of course, her name would be Amber – just like the color of her hair," or "His name is Joey – he's just like my brother, Joseph."

There are many ways that parents can validate their own feelings by honoring their children, but *naming* them can be one of the most important. The name affirms the significance of the loss and replaces the emptiness with a *restored identity.* For some women, the names come easily. For others, it may take a little longer. Some women struggle with guilt, feeling unworthy to name their children. It's important to remember that being perfect isn't a requirement for being a parent. A name is really a gift from God – a gift that that He has allowed us to bestow.

Through prayer, many grieving mothers are able to gain a sense of the names that God intends for their children.

Picturing the child with Jesus can be very comforting in the mourning process. We know that Jesus said, "Let the children come unto me." Knowing that he will not reject our children is consoling. Also, remembering the love and acceptance of Christ can help reduce any fears we might have of not being accepted by our children in Heaven.

Naming our children and picturing them with Jesus are important steps toward wholeness. Their completion gives form to what we know by faith. In the end, it is our union with God that gives substance to *all* our relationships. Below are some specific ways of putting these principles into practice.

1. Giving the baby a name: As mentioned above, prayer can give mothers and fathers a sense of *who their child is* and inspire them to think of an appropriate name. However, for those looking for additional resources, there are a number of good books available as well as online resources for baby names along with their meanings (try babyname.org). Dictionaries of the saints can be great reference tools, as well. Naming a child after a saint can help to reinforce a sense of the child being in Heaven and inspire confidence in those who would welcome the intercession and example of a special patron. The Bible is another great treasury of names, definitions and inspirational characters that you may want to consider. One of the advantages of naming a child in Heaven is that there is no need to worry about whether the name will be "popular" or if people will be able pronounce it. Parents can feel free to choose the name that they find most meaningful for their child – even if it happens to be Enoch or Haggai.

2. *Writing the letter:* Some people may want to do this more than once to express the feelings they've been holding in. Those who have more than one child often wish to write letters to each of them. Reading the letter (or letters) during a memorial service can be powerful, but reading them aloud to a therapist, a priest or a friend may help as well. Placing the letters in a scrapbook creates a tangible memory to cherish.

3. *Participating in Memorial Services and Commemorations:* Rachel's Vineyard™ offers an opportunity to honor the unborn child in a special service followed by a Mass. Letters, as mentioned above, are often read as a part of the memorial, but there are many symbolic options to choose from. Writing a poem, creating a plaque or planting a memorial garden (and having a private service *there*) are just a few examples of the special ways that the importance of the child could be demonstrated. Writing songs and painting pictures are wonderful forms of expression for those who are creative. Others may prefer something practical: making a donation to charity in the child's name can be a meaningful commemorative act.

4. *Connecting with other children:* This can be painful for women who haven't dealt with their losses. But once the grief has been acknowledged, restorative experiences with children can be powerful. If you don't have children of your own, sponsoring a child through a helping organization or volunteering to work with children can provide structured experiences for nurturing. Babysitting for friends or family can also provide a positive connection with young people.

5. ***Additional Reading:*** *I'll Hold You in Heaven,* by Jack Hayford (1986, 1990) is a book with Scriptural references that some women suffering from pregnancy loss have found to be a helpful and hope-filled resource.

Notes:

Notes:

Notes:

Notes:

Notes:

Notes:

Notes:

Chapter Three:
Reconnecting with God

One of the most painful after-effects of abortion is the feeling of isolation, not only from friends and family but also from God. Restoring our relationship with Him is essential. The following examples illustrate the impact of abortion on the spiritual life.

Thalia had an abortion when she was sixteen. She believed that it was wrong, but she believed that pre-marital sex was even worse. If she'd gone through with the pregnancy, she would have had to admit to her parents – and to her church – that she had sinned.

That wouldn't have been easy. Thalia was a preacher's daughter. She was expected to set an example. Her parents constantly reminded her of her position in the church: she had obligation to be a model for other young people there.

Thalia tried to live up to their demands. She was a soloist in the choir and a leader in the church youth group. She was always there for the car washes and doughnut sales, but more importantly, she had given talks to other teens on the importance of *chastity*. She knew how shocked everyone would be if they found out that she had become pregnant.

Thalia thought that having an abortion was her only way out of a difficult situation. She felt that God would forgive her for the abortion faster than the church would forgive her for getting pregnant.

She also reasoned that if others knew that she had "messed up," they might be more likely to get into trouble themselves. Her parents were always telling her that her life had an influence on others. Other girls at church copied the way that she dressed and modeled themselves after her behavior. If they knew that she'd had sex, perhaps they would follow her example

Her father, too, would be affected. She feared he might lose his job. Preachers were expected to manage their own children. She knew that there would be repercussions, though she didn't know what they would be. She convinced herself that an abortion was "the best thing for everyone," and she terminated the pregnancy before she started to show.

As it turned out, however, the abortion wasn't what was best for Thalia. She asked God to forgive her, but she still felt guilty and couldn't sleep at night. At church, when her father made the altar call each Sunday, she longed to go forward but wondered what other people would think if they saw her crying. There were several times when she felt especially "convicted." Her father's words seemed aimed directly at her. He said, "There are some of you right here in this church who have *sin* in their lives that only God sees. You may have been saved for years ... You may come to church every Sunday ... But if you think that no one knows what you've done, God knows ... and you need to come forward and repent."

Thalia couldn't come forward, however. She didn't want anyone asking any questions. That was the whole point of having the abortion in the first place: *not having to tell.* Keeping her secret was one motivation for staying in her pew. But she also began to wonder if God really could forgive her. Before she had gotten pregnant, pre-marital sex seemed to be the unforgivable sin, and the abortion was the only way she could "make it right." But the guilt from the abortion was even greater than the guilt she had felt over having sex. She couldn't imagine how she could ever be free from that.

Thalia carried her regrets alone for years. She quit going to church hoping to avoid the feelings of shame that inevitably arose. But then, she felt even more cut off from God.

Finally, a friend told her about a *Rachel Network Evening of Prayer* at a church she had never been to. Maria never dreamed that Thalia might have had an abortion. The service was open to anyone who had been affected by this issue. Maria told Thalia that she'd had an abortion years ago, and she wanted Thalia to go along with her for moral support.

Thalia agreed. No one there would know her secret – not even Maria. She was amazed that Maria had been willing to reveal something so private, but Thalia had no intention of returning her confidence.

When Thalia and Maria went to church that night, they both felt a sense of God's presence. This time, Thalia didn't feel His "wrath." Instead, there was an atmosphere of peace in the little chapel they entered. As she sat there in the pew with Maria, she closed her eyes and told the Lord all that she was feeling. For the first time in years, she felt comforted and consoled.

At the end of the service, there was an opportunity for private prayer with the pastor. The anonymity of being at a different church made it easier for Thalia to receive the help that she needed. Instead of walking down to the front of the church, she prayed in the back of the candlelit chapel. Even Maria didn't notice that she had tears in her eyes.

When it was her turn to speak to the pastor in the reconciliation room, she told him that she was from a different church, but she just needed someone to talk to. He said that was okay – he didn't seem to have any intention of trying to influence her to join his church. Thalia poured out her story and cried as he listened. After she finished, he reassured her of God's love for her and His mercy. Then, he offered to pray for Thalia, and she said yes. He asked God to allow her to experience His forgiveness and freedom in her life.

Thalia felt her burden lift as he extended his hands upward and prayed for peace and restoration. She couldn't remember ever feeling that close to God before. As a child, she had constantly tried to please Him in order to appease her parents. She had felt pressure and guilt. But now, for the first time in her life, she felt truly accepted by Him: not because she had met all His expectations, but because He loved her enough to forgive her and take her back after so many years.

Thalia's biggest fear had been that someone might find out about her abortion, but as she drove home with Maria, she didn't care if her friend knew or not. She decided to confide in her. Maria seemed surprised, but she was happy that Thalia had been able to get help, too. Neither of them said much, however. They both felt a quiet sense of peace.

A week later, Maria invited Thalia to go to church with her again. This time, it was for a regular Sunday service. Thalia decided that she would try it, and the Sunday after that, she went again. Eventually, she decided to become a permanent member of the church where she had rediscovered her relationship with God.

Thalia is no longer afraid to go to church. She has learned to see God as a loving, forgiving Father, instead of a parent whose expectations she can never quite meet. Now she knows that she can always talk to God and confide in Him.

Bethany had the opposite problem with her father. He didn't put any expectations on her, but he disappointed *all* her expectations of him. When Bethany was twelve, her father left, and she was crushed. She prayed every night that he would come back, and *when he didn't*, she felt abandoned by God, as well as her father. She stopped going to church when her parents' divorce was final.

Bethany had never asked God for anything before, and when He didn't bring her dad back, she felt that there was no point in praying at all. She told everyone that she no longer believed in God, but what really happened was that she stopped believing in *people*. She hated her father for leaving her mother and felt that, if she couldn't trust him, there was no one whom she *could* trust.

When Bethany started dating, she deliberately chose boys that she knew her father and mother would dislike. Whenever her mother expressed disapproval, she would throw the divorce up in her face. What did her mother know about choosing the right guy? Her father was supposed to be one of the "good ones," but their marriage had failed. Bethany wanted to find someone who was as different from her father as possible.

When she got pregnant, she didn't trust her parents enough to tell them about it. She was determined not to ask them for help or be judged by them. When her boyfriend refused to take responsibility for their child, she was even more adamant about not telling them – she didn't want to hear her mother say, "I told you so."

Bethany didn't really want to have an abortion. She wanted to keep her baby and be a better parent than her own parents had been to her. But that didn't seem possible under the circumstances. After it was over, she felt sad and angry. She was even angrier at her parents than before. She also felt angry at God – and *that* surprised her since she didn't even think that she believed in Him. She realized that she felt the same anger she had experienced when her parents divorced. It occurred to her that she had never really stopped believing in God: *she just stopped talking to Him.*

After the abortion, however, she started talking to Him a lot. She wanted to know why He would send her a baby when she had no way of taking care of it. There were lots of women who wanted children. There were women who tried to have babies and couldn't conceive. It didn't seem fair that she should have gotten pregnant without even trying – especially since she and her boyfriend had been using "protection."

And yet, she was also angry that God didn't do something to make it possible for her to *keep* her baby once she *did* get pregnant. Although she hadn't asked Him for help, He could have intervened anyway, she reasoned.

She was angry with God about the divorce. She didn't know why He let her father leave her, and she didn't know why He let her boyfriend abandon her when she needed him. A little voice inside told her that she should have listened to her mother, but that little voice made her even angrier. How could she have known that her mother was right about her boyfriend when she had been wrong about her dad?

It seemed to her that God and her parents had gotten her into a quagmire where there were no right choices and nothing made sense. Because of them, she felt that she had lost the only person who might truly have loved her: *her baby.*

None of Bethany's friends knew about the abortion (and she didn't want them to) so she had no one to talk to except God. She let Him have the brunt of all her anger. As she complained to Him, day after day, she began to experience some relief from her rage. God just listened. He never criticized her, as her mother had done, and He never seemed to go anywhere – unlike her father. Day after day, He was there for her.

Bethany had pulled away from most of her friends, but there were a few who stuck by her even when she tried to push them away. Jennifer was a Christian, and although Bethany thought that she was a little pushy with her beliefs, she was always there to answer Bethany's questions about God.

Bethany found out about the *Rachel Network Evening of Prayer* from Jennifer. Jennifer had brought home a bulletin from her church, and as she was reading through the events for the week, she noticed that there was a service for people who had been affected by abortion. Jennifer said that she had a friend who'd had an abortion, and she thought about going there on her behalf just to see what it was all about. She had no idea that Bethany would take her idea personally. But Bethany burst into tears when she mentioned it. At first, she was angry that Jennifer had even mentioned the word, "abortion." But as her emotions poured out, she felt a desire to tell her everything that she had been through.

Jennifer listened as Bethany told her story for the first time, and when she was finished, they cried together. Afterwards, Jennifer offered to pray with her, and Bethany agreed.

Jennifer prayed with a sense of assurance that Bethany envied. She had been so angry at God, for so long that it was hard for her to imagine having a good relationship with Him. Her anger had helped her to reconnect with her *belief* in God and had prompted her to talk to Him again. But it was keeping her from really getting close to Him. Jennifer, however, seemed to have a relationship with Him that was based on real love and trust – and Bethany wanted that too.

Sharing her story and praying with Jennifer helped to break down the barriers that were keeping her from getting to know God. Jennifer offered to go to the Evening of Prayer with her that very week, and Bethany said yes. It was the first time that Bethany had been in a church since her childhood. It brought back so many memories – some bad, but some good. It reminded her of a simpler time in her life when she trusted God and thought that her parents were perfect. She missed those days. However, as she listened to the soothing music and closed her eyes, she pictured herself with the Lord and felt closer to Him than she had even as a child. His love was unconditional. She realized that He was the *only one* who was perfect and that her expectations of her parents – and herself – had been unrealistic. She had given up her baby because she believed that she couldn't be *"good enough"* as a mother. And she had given up on her parents because they weren't "good enough" either. She had blamed God for all that had happened, but she had never really given Him a chance to meet her needs. She had never stepped out in faith – with a hand open to receive from Him and to give to someone else.

Trusting in God had seemed to be too much of a risk. However, she had reached a point in her life where relying on herself just wasn't enough. By staying angry at God, she had put herself in a precarious position. Everything in her life was up to her – and yet, she felt that she had failed herself as much as everyone else had.

She longed to have a deeper kind of relationship with God – one where she could turn to Him in times of stress and crisis and find comfort

At the Evening of Prayer, in the quiet of the church, she closed her eyes and pictured the Lord standing in front of her. As she gazed into His eyes, she felt close to Him for the first time. She made up her mind that she was no longer going to keep Him at arms length. She wanted to start over with Him and with everyone else in her life. As she prayed with Jennifer's pastor that night, she resolved to step out in faith and have a real relationship with God.

As the days went on, Bethany was surprised at how freeing it was to trust in God – to rely on Him instead of herself. She no longer felt guilty about not being "perfect." And she found that her anger towards her parents diminished too. She didn't need them to be "perfect" either.

When Bethany allowed herself to open up to her friend, Jennifer, it helped her to open up to God. And once she opened up to God, He helped her to open up to other people. Now, Bethany has started to let others into her life. She doesn't worry so much about whether or not they are going to let her down. She has found support from someone Who is never going to abandon or forsake her. Now that

Bethany knows she can trust God, she finds it easier to trust her friends and herself – knowing that His love will be there to fill in the gaps.

Kira never knew her father. He left before she was even born. Her mother dated lots of men after that. Some of them even moved in, but none of them ever stayed for very long.

Kira grew up without ever being told about God. Her mother didn't go to church and Kira didn't really know anyone who did. Sometimes she heard other children at school talking about their youth groups at church or their Bible studies, but Kira never got close enough to them to ask any questions. She wasn't really comfortable around other children because she was shy. She had a hard time making friends, and the fact that her mother didn't allow her to invite guests over after school didn't make things any easier.

Kira's first friendship was with her boyfriend in high school. He was a senior and she was just a freshman. The age difference didn't bother her – she had always felt more comfortable with people older than herself.

Bobby introduced her to other people at school, and Kira felt accepted for the first time in her life. She began looking to her boyfriend and his friends for the guidance that she had never gotten from her mother.

When Kira got pregnant, Bobby was the first person she told. He didn't seem to have any hesitation about the situation. He knew exactly where to go to the get the abortion. It all happened so quickly that Kira didn't have time to think. But she trusted Bobby more than she'd ever trusted anyone in her life, and she went along with his advice.

She didn't question his judgment – not even when she realized how wrong he had been to promise her that the abortion would be painless. It was excruciating, and after it was over, she had a difficult time recovering from the procedure.

But the physical pain wasn't the worst part. Almost as soon as they left the clinic, Bobby's attitude towards her changed. He became distant. A few weeks later, she found out that he was seeing one of the girls who claimed to be "just a friend" of his. She began to realize that many of her newfound friends were really just girls who were waiting for a chance to go out with Bobby. None of them really cared about her.

Kira was devastated when she realized the truth. It had never occurred to her that she would lose Bobby. She thought that they were going to be together forever. Having a baby with him would have been a dream come true. She had always wanted a family of her own, and once Bobby was gone, she desperately wanted their baby back again.

She had no one to turn to for support or reassurance. She wanted to die and tried cutting her wrists, but it didn't work. She bled a little, but no one noticed.

After that, Kira just went through the motions at school. She didn't date, and she didn't have any friends. Her grades plummeted, but she didn't care.

As the years passed, she continued to grieve over Bobby and the loss of their child. She had no idea how to get help. She sought treatment for depression, but never got any better. Finally, she began looking for answers on the Internet. She started going to chat rooms and websites for support and advice about her mood problems. One night, when she was online, a woman shared about her abortion and mentioned that she had found help through Rachel's Vineyard™. Kira had thought that she was the only woman in the world who had difficulty dealing with her abortion. She was surprised to find that there were many other women who were grieving too.

Kira went to the Rachel's Vineyard™ website and, after reading more about it, she decided that she wanted to go on a retreat. She didn't know exactly what to expect, but she was tired of suffering alone.

As she drove to the retreat center she was nervous, but the minute she walked through the door, she was glad she had come. As she met the other women, it was reassuring to know that they shared a common experience. But what was really comforting to Kira was something that she had not expected: the presence of God.

Kira was the only one there who had never been to church. The only thing she knew about Jesus was that he had something to do with Christmas and Easter. But at her house, the holidays had been nothing more than an opportunity for her mother to get drunk.

No one had ever told her about God – or that Jesus was alive and that he loved her. Some of the women at the retreat were angry at God. They had been to church and had been hurt there. But to Kira, it was all new. She was overjoyed to encounter Christ as a real person who cared about her – who would never abandon her the way that others had.

At the retreat, she found real friends for the first time in her life. They understood her pain and, with their support, she found solace in her grief over the loss of her child. Yet, for Kira, the most important thing was the relationship that she found with God. This was the love that she had looked for all her life. That weekend – and in the weeks following the retreat – she began to feel complete and whole in this new relationship where God's love filled the emptiness that she had lived with for so long.

C*ecilia* didn't like to think about the subject of abortion. She didn't believe that it was the kind of thing that should be talked about in polite society. Whenever anyone mentioned the word, she became angry – especially when they preached about it at church. What she really wanted was for the pastor to stand at the pulpit and tell all the parents to start watching their children more carefully. If young people didn't have pre-marital sex, she thought, there would be no abortions, and no one would have to talk about it anymore. The real problem was teenagers whose parents weren't looking after them.

Cecilia had three daughters in their teens, and she kept a strict watch over their behavior. They came to church every Sunday and Wednesday night along with Cecilia's husband, Victor. Their sixteen-year-old daughter was allowed to date, but only in groups with other people from church.

All their daughters were accomplished and well-behaved. Everyone thought that they had the perfect family, and they gave Cecilia most of the credit for that. The other women in the church looked up to her – she seemed to handle everything so well. When people dropped by her house unexpectedly, it was always immaculate. She made time to volunteer for church activities. At funerals and bake sales and covered dish dinners, Cecilia was the first to show up with a cake or casserole – and afterwards, everyone wanted her recipe.

Cecilia thought that her life was just as perfect as everyone else believed. But all that changed when her husband announced that he was leaving her for another woman. Cecilia was in shock.

She thought that things couldn't get any worse, but a few days after her husband moved out, she took a home pregnancy test that came out positive. The thought of having a baby again, after so many years, might have been daunting under the best of circumstances, but the thought of going through it without a husband was devastating. Her morning sickness lasted all day, and her hormones made it harder to hold back the tears when she thought about the loss of her marriage. She wanted to be strong for her daughters, but she was depressed and couldn't think clearly.

In spite her situation, however, having an abortion never occurred to her until her sister suggested it. Lucy was the only one that Cecilia confided in during the divorce. Her friends from church were Victor's friends, too, and they didn't want to alienate him by "taking Cecilia's side." Cecilia didn't want that either. She hoped that Victor would stay in church, so she stepped back to avoid causing any conflicts. She withdrew from their mutual friends so he would feel that he could confide in them. Not all of her friends at church were close to Victor. The women from the Ladies Auxiliary didn't have any real excuse for distancing themselves, but they were uncomfortable with her situation. They didn't know how to offer their support, and Cecilia felt too embarrassed to admit that she needed their help.

In the absence of all her friends from church, Cecilia turned to her family. She and Lucy had never been close before. They had different beliefs about almost everything, and this had caused many conflicts over the years. But the real root of their discord was Lucy's jealousy. She had been envious of Cecilia since they were children, and she became very resentful when Cecilia got married before she did. Her sister's perfect marriage infuriated her – especially when her own relationships always seemed to fail.

When Cecilia's life started to come apart, the envy evaporated, and that relieved one source of tension between the two of them. When Cecilia admitted to her sister that she was pregnant, Lucy quickly suggested that she "have it taken care of." At first, Cecilia didn't know what she was talking about. Neither of them had ever discussed abortion, before – it made her uncomfortable just to say the word. Cecilia would have been mortified to talk to her doctor about it. However, Lucy didn't give up. She assured Cecilia that she didn't *ever* need to tell her doctor what happened. There were places she could go anonymously – where she could be treated by a doctor she would never see again.

Cecilia still believed that abortion was wrong, but she was too sick and too desperate to argue with her sister. After all, Lucy was the one person who was willing to "be there" for her. She didn't want to give up her child, but Lucy reminded her that she had three other children to think of. Cecilia wasn't even sure how she was going to care for them. When Lucy asked her how she could possibly manage with a newborn in the house, she had no answer.

Cecilia thought about telling Victor, but Lucy discouraged her. The possibility of a new baby would put too much pressure on him, she said, and if Cecilia told him the truth, it would ruin any chance of reconciliation.

Cecilia finally gave in to Lucy's urging and terminated the pregnancy. She didn't feel guilty right away. At first, she was just relieved that it was over. By the time the self-recriminations set in a few weeks later, she was already feeling guilty about everything *else* in her life, and the abortion was just one more drop in the ocean.

She felt guilty and ashamed that her marriage had failed. Although she had been considered a model wife and mother, she felt that people looked at her differently once she became a single mom. In fact, her own daughters seemed to look at her differently – blaming her for their father's departure.

Cecilia was forced to get a job when Victor left, and this caused an even greater rift between her and the girls. They had been so carefully protected, but after the divorce, they were on their own much of the time. She worried about them and felt guilty, but there was nothing she could do to change the situation. Her life became so hectic that she found it harder to get to church on Sundays. She had initially stepped back so that Victor wouldn't feel uncomfortable. Then, she missed services because she didn't have time. Eventually, she stayed away because she didn't want to encounter people's questions or their looks.

If she could have gotten angry at Victor, she probably would have felt less depressed. But, after the abortion, she felt that she couldn't hold him accountable for anything he'd done to her. Although her decision to terminate the pregnancy had been made, in part, to protect him from feeling pressured, she still felt guilty for taking his child away. In her mind, her sin seemed far worse than his, and so she took all the blame on herself for everything that had happened.

She accused herself of being a hypocrite. She had never really judged people who had gotten divorced or had abortions. But she had distanced herself from them. By refusing to talk about subjects that she considered unpleasant or impolite, she had done the same thing to others that her friends had done to her. She had closed the door to any discussions that might have allowed people to confide in her about their struggles.

Cecilia's regrets loomed in the back of her mind for years. They created a barrier that kept her from going to God with all of her problems. For a long time, the guilt was greater than the grief. However, once her daughters were grown, she began to think about the child she had lost. By then, her life wasn't so hectic anymore. She was alone, much of the time, in an empty house. For the first time, she wished that her youngest child – who would have been five by then – could still have been with her.

She wished that she could pray, but she didn't know how to start. When she looked back on her life, she realized that she had never really felt close to God. She had always tried to "do the right things" to please Him – to be a good wife and mother. But when "all the right things" didn't work anymore, her relationship with God seemed to vanish, and she didn't know how to find it again.

One day, a friend told her about the *Rachel Network Evening of Prayer.* Her friend said that she knew several people who'd had abortions, and she was going there to pray for them. She asked Cecilia to come along, not wanting to go alone, but never dreaming it might be an issue for Cecilia too.

Cecilia agreed to go along for support – even though she was afraid to go back into a church after so many years. She was nervous when they first arrived, but once she sat down in the pew, it felt good to be there in spite of her fears.

Cecilia had gone to church all her life and had heard hundreds of sermons about God's forgiveness. In theory, she believed that He was merciful, but she had never really put that principle to the test. In the past, when she prayed the Lord's Prayer and asked God to "forgive us our trespasses," it was usually *other* people's trespasses that came to mind. It wasn't until the divorce that she began to feel a sense of her own sin.

Because of the divorce, she had been feeling guilty even *before* she had the abortion. She had already started to question whether she was a good mother or not. The feeling that she had "failed" somehow, led her to believe that she didn't deserve another child. And that belief led to the choice that she later regretted.

At the Evening of Prayer, Cecilia began to look at her guilt in a new way. She realized that she wasn't the only one to blame. She had never acknowledged her anger towards Victor – or towards anyone else for that matter. She thought that "forgiveness" meant not being angry. But it occurred to her that she couldn't really *forgive* if she never acknowledged that she had been hurt in the first place. As she thought back over the events surrounding the divorce and the abortion, it struck her that there were many people who had hurt her: Victor, who had left her without warning, and all the friends who stood aloof when she needed them.

She also realized that she was angry at her sister, Lucy. After the abortion, Lucy had disappeared from her life, again. Cecilia had always wondered why her sister had bothered to reconnect with her when she had no intention of standing by her. At the time, she had given Lucy the benefit of the doubt, wanting to believe that she had cared for her in her moment of crisis. Yet, in retrospect, she began to question Lucy's intentions.

Lucy had always resented her, and perhaps it been unwise for her to believe that she had Cecilia's best interests at heart. Cecilia had never blamed her sister for the abortion, knowing that the decision had been her own. But she finally admitted that she was angry with her for pressuring her when she was so vulnerable. Lucy's urging had really gone beyond the boundaries of concerned advice. She had called Cecilia on the phone late at night, more than once, and had wakened her early in the morning, pressing her to go with her to the clinic. If Cecilia had not been so distraught, she probably would have just said, "No, thank you," and hung up the phone. But in her debilitated condition, that kind of persuasion had a powerful impact.

For the first time, it occurred to her that Lucy might have had an abortion herself. She had been surprisingly knowledgeable about the procedure: where to go, how to get one, and how "easy" it was. Perhaps Lucy had been suffering, too, with the same pain that Cecilia had endured all these years.

She forgave Lucy, and then she forgave Victor, too, after acknowledging, for the first time, that she was angry with him for what he had done. She forgave her friends. And finally, she forgave herself.

Once she let her anger out, she was able to turn to God again. She realized that she had been harboring anger against Him, too. She had kept Him at a distance instead of acknowledging the real sources of her pain. Once she stopped pretending, she was able to open up to God and let Him be a part of her life again. She asked Him for His forgiveness and felt His love in a way that she had never experienced before.

When the service was over, Cecilia felt a newfound strength inside. Now that she was at peace with God, she felt ready to move on with her life. Although she still felt the loss of the people she had let go of, she knew that she would never lose the one relationship that mattered most. She no longer felt that God's love was based on her ability to "do everything right." She had acknowledged how she felt and who she really was before Him. As a result, she felt closer to God than ever before.

Cate lived in the desert and was wakened every morning by the sound of the *Call to Prayer*. The chanting became familiar, and she respected the faith of the people around her, but she had no desire to join them. Before moving overseas, she had grown up among friends and family who considered themselves too intellectual for religion. In their milieu, God was never discussed. To Cate, the faith of others seemed primitive and exotic. It was interesting, but it had no place inside of her. She didn't feel the need for God until after her abortion. In her grief, she wanted to believe in God so that she could believe in Heaven, too. She wanted to know that her baby was alive and at peace. She went on a Rachel's Vineyard Retreat™ hoping to find a connection between this life and the next. On the last morning of the retreat, she got up early and walked on the beach. There in the sand, she wrote a letter to God and to her baby. As the waves washed over the words, she felt the distance between herself and Heaven melting into the greatness of the sea. After being in the desert for so long, the immense water seemed even more powerful and made her realize how thirsty she had been – for something deep and intangible to give life to her soul. Despite the pain of her loss, she felt a sense of awe and gratitude that her baby had led her to the God who seemed so distant for so many years.

Scripture for Meditation:

"If anyone is thirsty, let him come to me and drink."
(John 7:37)

"Everyone who drinks this water will be thirsty again, but whoever drinks the water that I give will never be thirsty. For the water I give shall become a fountain within, leaping up to provide eternal life." (John 4:13-14)

"A man had two sons. The younger of them said to his father, 'Give me the share of the estate that is mine.' So the father divided up the property. Several days later, this son collected all his possessions and went off to a distant land where he squandered his money on dissolute living. After he had spent everything, a great famine broke out in that country, and he was in desperate need. So he attached himself to one of the landed class of the place who sent him to his farm to take care of the pigs. He longed to feed himself with the husks that were fodder for the pigs, but no one made a move to give him anything. Coming to his senses, at last, he said: 'How many hired hands at my father's place have more than enough to eat, while here, I am starving. I will leave and return to my father, and say to him: 'Father, I have sinned against God and against you; I no longer deserve to be called your son. Treat me like one of your hired hands.' With that he set off for his father's house. While he was still a long way off, his father caught sight of him and was deeply moved. He ran out to meet him, threw his arms around his neck, and kissed him. The son said to him, "Father, I have sinned against God, and against you; I no longer deserve to be called your son.'

The father said to his servants: 'Hurry! Bring out the finest robe and put it on him. Put a ring on his finger and shoes on his feet. Take the fatted calf and kill it. Let us eat and celebrate because this son of mine was dead and has come back to life. He was lost and is found.' Then the celebration began." (Luke 15:11-24)

"Come to me, all you who are weary and burdened, and I will give you rest." (Matthew 11:28)

"All that the Father gives me will come to me, and whoever comes to me I will never reject." (John 6:37)

Prayer:

Father, You are the only perfect parent who can truly meet our needs. Your love for us knows no bounds. Jesus told us the story of the Prodigal Son to show Your fatherly compassion for Your children. When the son who had left returned to his father, he was not greeted with questions or recriminations. In fact, his father didn't even wait for him to apologize. It was enough to know that his child needed him. His son had come back because he was hungry and exhausted. He was tired of living without dignity among people who didn't care about him.

When we find ourselves tired at the end of the day, longing for more out of life to meet the deep thirst and hunger of our souls, You are ready to take us back. You rejoice in having Your children restored to You. When we have lost our dignity by trusting in people who don't care for us or respect us, You long to restore the honor and the love that we have lost.

When we return to You, after running away, we are not met with criticism and condemnation. Your arms are always open to embrace us and to guide us as we renew our relationship with You.   Amen.

Review of Practical Suggestions:

1. Keep current on post-abortion recovery events. Rachel's Vineyard™ is offered all year long in the United States and in many locations worldwide. If you don't have it in your area, you can find the nearest one at http://www.rachelsvineyard.org. Don't worry if there isn't one close by. Many women actually prefer going out of their own area for extra anonymity. The *Rachel Network Evening of Prayer* is available in book form and on videotape. To order, visit http://www.rachelnetwork.org.
.

2.   Visualize children with Christ on an ongoing basis. Picturing our little ones in Heaven with the Lord not only relieves fears about our children's happiness and well-being, it reveals God in a tender and gentle light.   When we see the Lord cradling a little child or infant lovingly, it's impossible to view him with an angry or vengeful face. The *Rachel Network Evening of Prayer* allows time for this exercise, but some women choose to do it regularly – long after the evening is over.

3. Cultivate personal daily prayer. Structured prayers can be surprisingly powerful when we are at a loss for words with God. The Divine Mercy prayers are a great resource.

Scripture can also help. The Psalms are full of prayers that express a wide range of emotions. The verses in this book – along with other passages that focus on God's mercy, love and forgiveness – can be pondered in meditation. When talking to God, *honesty* is important. There's no point in pretending that we're not angry or sad. God knows how we feel already – He just wants to hear it from us! For those who find it difficult to talk to God, writing a letter may be a good option.

4. *Participate in the Sacraments.* The signs and symbols that accompany these occasions of healing provide rituals, which research has found to be important with post-abortion recovery. The grace conferred can help to bring about wholeness as we connect with God more deeply.

(A.) *Confession:* Pope John Paul II has made a special effort to reach out to women who may be fearful about returning to the sacraments:

> *I would now like to say a special word to women who have had an abortion …. The wound in your heart may not yet have healed …. But do not give into discouragement and do not lose hope …. The Father of mercies is ready to give you His forgiveness and His peace in the Sacrament of Reconciliation (Par. 99).*

Both Rachel's Vineyard™ and the *Rachel Network Evening of Prayer* provide opportunities for the Sacrament of Reconciliation. However, Confession in any setting can be helpful. Therapists and ministers involved in post-abortion healing may want to recommend priests whom they know to be particularly sensitive to this issue. A compassionate confessor can create a sense of offering "permission" to feel forgiven. There is something particularly comforting in having the reassurance of mercy from someone perceived as God's representative.

For some women, this sacrament may be the first step towards healing – and the most difficult one to take! Some are so fearful of having to confess the abortion that they avoid church for years afterward. Others confess the abortion over and over again without feeling forgiven. It's important to remember that we *are* forgiven, even if we don't *feel it,* after being absolved.

It may also be useful to look at what's keeping us stuck in feelings of guilt. One common reason for this is that the reconciliation with God is only *one* piece of the healing. Other steps are necessary, too.

Though Confession is intended to reconnect us with the *whole community*, the focus in the sacrament is on God. Many women don't feel reconciled to others, to their children or to themselves, and negative feelings about these unresolved issues cause them to conclude that they are not forgiven. Going to Confession is one very important part of the healing process. It allows us to access God's grace for assistance in completing the additional steps towards wholeness and restoration.

(B.) *The Sacrament of the Anointing of the Sick:* After discussing the abortion in the confessional, some women may wish to request this sacrament. There can be physical as well as spiritual healing in the anointing, along with an increase of *confidence* in divine mercy. You may want to discuss this with your priest.

(C.) *Communion:* Frequent reception of the Eucharist is a wonderful way to experience God's love and restoration. Many women miss out on this after an abortion because they feel unworthy. However, it's important not to let *feelings* of guilt stand in the way. After going to confession, it's good to receive the fullness of grace in Communion as soon as possible. Regular reception of the sacraments will help to facilitate the healing process. If daily Communion is possible, this can be of great benefit.

Note to Priests: There are a number of important issues for post-abortive women regarding the Sacraments and participation at church. *The Jericho Plan: Breaking Down the Walls Which Prevent Post-Abortion Healing* **(Reardon, 1996) is a good resource with practical suggestions for clergy. You may also want to consider the following:**

(A.) *Confession* is an ideal time to promote post-abortion healing. Even after receiving absolution, many women need additional support systems in order to feel forgiven. Some women will continue to seek out different priests and repeatedly confess the abortion because of persistent, negative, unresolved emotions. You may want to address this directly by reassuring them that, though their *feelings* may still take some time to heal, the *truth* is that God has forgiven them. Let them know that the door is open to speak with you again – or with someone you recommend.

Another way to address this issue is to give out brochures or business cards after Confession. Your diocesan Respect Life Office should be able to provide you with local contact numbers for post-abortion healing.

Check with them to see what's offered in your area. Additionally, the Rachel's Vineyard™ website (http://www.rachelsvineyard.org) can be a great way to help women reconnect. Rachel's Vineyard has some options for women to have contact with "e-mail buddies" who can provide support.

In addition to giving out information personally, you can also keep brochures in the literature rack to reach out to women who might be tentative about coming back to church or talking to a priest face to face.

Some women have difficulty with Confession because they believe that they are permanently excommunicated and ineligible even for the Sacrament of Reconciliation. Without dwelling too much on this issue with penitents (who may or may not have heard this misrepresentation of Canon Law), it's important to reassure those who receive absolution that they are *completely forgiven.* Even if they don't feel forgiven right away, they are free to share in the sacramental life of the Church.

On the other end of the spectrum, you may encounter women who have continued to receive Communion after their abortion without going to Confession at all. These women may never have received sufficient instruction in the faith to know that the Sacrament of Reconciliation was a necessary step.

It's also important to consider that not all women are culpable for the abortions they underwent. Some women report being sedated and restrained without ever giving consent. Even in cases where there is some acquiescence, women may have been coerced and pressured to the point that they felt they had no choice in the matter.

In either case, it is important to reassure women of God's mercy, and encourage them to come back and talk if they need to. Going to Communion as soon possible after receiving absolution (before the guilt and fear set in again) can help to break the cycle of shame that keeps women away from the Church.

(B.) *Sacrament of the Anointing of the Sick.* For a discussion of health issues and the applicability of the anointing, see the Appendix for Priests.

(C.) *Prayer.* Praying aloud with men and women who come seeking God's love is powerful. After being distanced from God and the Church, some people simply don't know *how* to pray anymore. Hearing a priest or minister address God and ask Him to meet their needs can be very healing and may help to jump-start the prayers of a person feeling alienated from the Lord. Offer to pray with those who ask for your help. It's great to pray *for* people, but praying *together* can bring others into God's presence.

Notes:

Notes:

Notes:

Notes:

Notes:

Notes:

Notes:

Chapter Four:
Reconnecting with Ourselves

One of the most painful myths about abortion is the idea that it is a *self-centered* choice. In reality, it is often a wrenching sacrifice made to satisfy the needs or demands of others. One of the most important connections to be re-established in the healing process is the connection with the *self*. Prior to the pregnancy, there may have been many forms of coercion that preceded the pressure to abort. A habit of yielding to the desires of others (at the expense one's own needs) can produce a pattern of compromise and self-violation.

Healing after the termination of a pregnancy involves a rediscovery of core emotional needs and the deeper aspirations of the heart.

Ronelle tried to get back to her regular routine as soon as possible after her abortion. On Sunday, she went to church, as usual. She wasn't expecting to find the joy that she previously had – her nerves were too raw for that – but she had hoped that it might distract her from the pain for just an hour or two. Instead, she found herself in even greater distress. Her pastor gave a sermon about the selfishness of the modern world and cited abortion as one of the worst examples. He painted a vivid picture of women who had abortions because they didn't want to interrupt their ski vacations or their summers at the beach.

His words were devastating to Ronelle. She felt judged and misunderstood. But there was no way that she could defend herself to her pastor without telling him something that she hadn't even told her husband, Mitch.

Ronelle had wanted her baby desperately, but Mitch was out of work and was suffering from depression. The three children they already had seemed to be more than he could handle. Ronelle had feared that the pressure of another child would push him over the edge.

She didn't tell him about her abortion because she wanted to spare him the grief that she was feeling. However, after it was over, she wondered if she had made the right decision. Her only relief was reminding herself that she had done it out of love for Mitch. Her pastor's remarks robbed her of that comfort. She knew that he wasn't really talking to her personally, but she felt as if he were pointing his finger at her the whole time he preached.

After that, Ronelle couldn't bring herself to go back to church. She was afraid of what she would hear. Going to church had been an important part of her life – but after the abortion, it became just one more part of herself that she felt she had to give up.

It wasn't until years later that she finally had the courage to set foot in a church again. A friend of hers invited her to a *Rachel Network Evening of Prayer*. She had a hard time believing that she could go to church without being judged, but she really wanted to try it. Her church had been her home away from home, and her heart ached when she thought of all she had missed through the years. Singing in the choir and worshipping with her husband and children had been her greatest joy. In spite of all the problems that they'd had, she longed to get her old life back again. Church had been their refuge.

For Ronelle, the Evening of Prayer was a first step towards reclaiming the life she missed. All she really wanted was to be able to sit down in a pew, again, without feeling condemned. But as she stood in the church singing *Amazing Grace,* she realized that the condemnation she was feeling wasn't coming from her old pastor or from God – it was coming from herself. Staying away from church had not protected her from feeling guilty. She realized that, by depriving herself of what she really wanted, she had been punishing herself all those years.

That night, she finally decided to let go of her guilt and forgive herself. She even decided to tell her husband about what had happened. She was afraid that he would be furious with her, but instead, he was relieved to finally understand what was wrong. He had always felt guilty for needing so much emotional support from Ronelle. He was glad to be able to support *her* for a change. Mitch had gotten counseling because of his depression, and that had helped him. He encouraged Ronelle to do the same. It was hard for her to admit that she needed help – she had been holding everything in for so long – but, in the end, it was a relief. Now, Ronelle is finally exploring the feelings and needs that she neglected when she made her difficult choice so many years before.

Lisa didn't really want to become sexually active in high school. But she loved her boyfriend and was more concerned about his needs than her own. When she found out she was pregnant, she wanted to have the baby and marry him, but she knew he wasn't ready for that.

Her only hope was her parents. When she told them that she was pregnant, they said that it was "okay," but they didn't see how they could help her take care of a baby. Although her mother didn't have a career, she was busy with volunteer work and charity functions. She didn't have time to be a grandmother. Lisa also sensed that her mother was embarrassed by the pregnancy. No one in their neighborhood had babies outside of wedlock – if they got pregnant at all, they got rid of the evidence quickly.

Lisa's father seemed understanding at first. He said that he would support Lisa no matter what ... but he didn't see how they could afford a baby. He was sure that her boyfriend would never be able to pay child support, and he feared that Lisa's brother might have to quit college if they had another child to drain their savings.

And what about the child, her mother wondered? What kind of life could he or she possibly have? Wasn't it selfish to bring a baby into the world under these circumstances?

That was the final straw for Lisa. She couldn't bear the idea of hurting everyone she loved – including her own child. Having the abortion was the biggest sacrifice she had ever made. She did it for her brother, her boyfriend, her baby, and for her parents. She did it for everyone except herself. For *her*, it was the loss of everything she ever wanted.

After it was over, everyone else acted as if nothing had happened. Lisa tried to go on with life as usual, but nothing was the same. She cried every night for months and lost interest in school and her other activities.

When the time came to apply for college, she didn't want to go. Looking at the tuition costs in the catalogs made her angry. How could her parents afford tens of thousands of dollars for her education when they had been worried about buying diapers for her baby? She had been willing to sacrifice her child for her brother's future – and for her boyfriend's future as well – but she couldn't live with herself if she felt that her baby had sacrificed his life for *her*.

Her only recourse when her parents insisted that she go to college was to make sure that she didn't succeed. She partied every night instead of studying, and by the end of the semester, she was put on academic probation.

She felt certain her parents wouldn't make her go back, after that, but they were *adamant*. They even offered her money if she would improve her grades.

Lisa went back to school determined to fail. She knew that if she didn't pull her grades up after Christmas break, she would have to leave – and that was exactly what she wanted. But shortly after the start of classes, a friend told her about Rachel's Vineyard™. Her roommate confided that she'd had an abortion in high school but had found healing by going on the retreat. Lisa was very surprised to learn that there were other women who were hurting just as she was. She had never heard anyone talk about her abortion before that. She found it hard to believe that a weekend retreat could change anything, but she decided to try it and see.

Her roommate quickly got online and found a one scheduled for that very weekend. It was six hours away, but she offered to go with Lisa and share the driving.

The long trip in the car gave Lisa plenty of time to get nervous. She was glad to have someone there for support. The hardest part was walking through the door of the retreat center and introducing herself. She tried to act cool and aloof – just as she did for parties and dates. She also tried to tell herself that she had no expectations and didn't really care what happened. But deep down, she was hoping for a miracle.

That evening, as the candles were lit, and they listened to the soft music in the background, Lisa thought about what she *really wanted* for the first time in a long time. Suddenly, her desires and needs came rushing into her mind: she wanted to be a mother; she wanted to roll back time and make a different choice for herself and her baby. She wanted to wait until she was really ready to go college – and not get a degree just because it was what her parents wanted. She wanted to take the time that she needed to heal.

During the retreat she wrote a letter to her parents to tell them how she felt. She was angry – but she was tired of letting her anger get in the way of living her life. On Sunday night, when she went back to campus, she called her parents and read her letter to them over the phone.

They were surprised by her feelings. But they still didn't want her to come home – they had already paid for her tuition. Lisa, however, pointed out that they could get a partial refund if she withdrew right away, but they wouldn't get anything back if she flunked out again. And she simply wasn't ready to concentrate on her studies. Without knowing what she wanted to do with her life, she couldn't find the motivation to succeed at school.

Her parents reluctantly agreed that coming home was the best decision. However, they stipulated that Lisa would need to get a job. Lisa was relieved. Her old job back home didn't pay a lot, but she felt that working would be a relief compared to school. Her parents also told her that they wanted her to get counseling, and she agreed to that as well. Actually, she was glad that her parents suggested this. She needed someone to talk to – in a way that she had never been able to talk to her family.

Now, Lisa is finally taking time to find out what she wants in life. She is reconnecting with the part of herself that she had lost. As she has grown in her understanding of her own needs, her anger towards her parents has finally begun to diminish.

Morgan lived her whole life trying to please everyone else. Even as a baby, she seemed to have an instinctive sense of how to placate and appease. As she grew, she learned to smooth things over between her parents when they fought. She distracted them with her smiles and her questions and made them forget their conflicts.

As she got older, however, their arguments became more heated, and she couldn't fix things between them anymore. Instead, she tried to calm her younger brothers when her parents' disagreements escalated. She would take them to her room and sing to them when Mom and Dad raised their voices.

When she was thirteen, they finally got divorced. This meant new responsibilities for Morgan along with her old ones. She had always helped out at home, but when her mother had to go to work, it became a serious obligation.

Morgan had to walk her brothers home from school and take care of them until dinnertime when her mother came home. Sometimes she didn't get home in time, so Morgan cooked and did the dishes. Although, her mom worked long hours, she didn't make much money, and so Morgan started earning cash on weekends to supplement their income. Instead of going to the mall with her friends or participating in sports, Morgan worked for the other mothers in the neighborhood. As a baby-sitter, she quickly gained the reputation of being mature and responsible. All the little children in the neighborhood loved her.

She worked hard at school, but it was tough to keep her grades up when she had so little time for studying. After high school, she wanted to go to a four-year college but didn't think that her academic record was good enough. Besides, her family needed her, and she didn't have time to waste on classes when she could be out there working and making money.

Morgan didn't want to become a nursing assistant, but the program was short and gave her enough training to make a little more income than her mother earned. And taking care of people came naturally to her.

It wasn't until she finished school that she started to date. She never had time for a social life or a boyfriend before. All that changed, however, when she met Eddie. If he hadn't needed her so much, she probably wouldn't have made time for him either, but he was the son of a patient she had cared for. Eddie's mother had asked Morgan to "look after him" once she was gone, and Morgan couldn't say no. She was always willing to help anyone in need.

Eddie was someone who really needed her. Although he was a grown man, he had never taken care of himself. His mother cooked his meals and made his bed for him until she became bedridden herself. Without Morgan, he would have been lost after her death. Morgan stepped in and filled the void. He asked her to move in with him, and she did. She took over all his mother's old responsibilities, just as she had taken on *her* mother's and father's responsibilities as a child. But this time, it was even more rewarding – because *this time,* she had a home of her own. She had a man who said that he loved her and was willing to live with her – unlike her father. And best of all, for the first time, she had no one else to defer to. Eddie was needy but he treated her with respect. All in all, she was happier than she had ever been before.

She was so content with her new life that she didn't think too much about the future. She believed that *someday* she and Eddie would get married, but she wasn't in a hurry.

Morgan didn't plan on getting pregnant, but when it happened, she wasn't unhappy. She had spent so many years taking care of other people's children that she was excited about the idea of finally having a child of her own. And she thought that Eddie would be a great father.

When Eddie found out, however, he was distraught. The idea of sharing Morgan's attention with someone else made him panic. He was afraid of what would happen if Morgan had to take time off from work – or even quit her job altogether. He certainly couldn't support a family.

Morgan promised him that the baby wouldn't be a "problem" for him. She was used to working and taking care of other people, and she was sure that she could manage a baby without much help from Eddie. It occurred to her that maybe her mother would help out. After, all, she had assisted her for years, taking care of her little brothers and working to help out with the finances. Now, her brothers were grown, and her mother had time on her hands. Morgan thought that she might enjoy having a grandchild to fill the empty hours.

Her mother didn't respond as she had hoped, however. The look on her face was one of shock and then outrage when Morgan told her the news. She felt too young to be a grandmother. And she certainly wasn't prepared to have a child in the house again. She told Morgan that she was crazy to even think about having a baby with Eddie. They were both too young. They should be enjoying life, at their age – not taking on more responsibility. She told her that getting pregnant too early had ruined her relationship with Morgan's father.

When Morgan's mother told her that getting pregnant had destroyed her marriage, Morgan was guilt-stricken. She remembered all her efforts as a child to solve her parents' problems. She had never thought of *herself* as the problem. But she was their firstborn – if they weren't ready for a baby, she felt that she must have hurt their marriage more than she helped it.

Morgan concluded that, by having a baby now, she would be sabotaging her mother's second chance at happiness. And she was worried about how Eddie would be affected as well. She didn't want to ruin his life by forcing him to be a father before he was ready. Morgan decided to have an abortion. No matter how much she wanted to be a mother, she decided that it wasn't worth hurting the people she loved.

Afterwards, she tried to put the pregnancy out of her mind. She still had Eddie, and she told herself that he was worth the sacrifice. She tried to convince herself that they were both better off without a baby in their lives.

As time went on though, she regretted her decision more and more. Even without the pressure of a baby, Eddie was overwhelmed by the daily demands of life, and nothing Morgan ever did seemed to be enough. She cooked his meals and let him drive her car. She made the payments on the house that he inherited from his mother, and paid for his health insurance. But Eddie still didn't want to get married. He didn't want to think about the future at all. And the truth was: *he didn't have to*. He had Morgan. She took care of everything for him.

Morgan, however, began to feel less and less hopeful about the future. She feared that she would never be a mother. Eddie kept promising that they could have children "someday." But she could see that he really didn't want to be a father. She stuck by him, though, hoping that he would have a change of heart.

Sometimes she thought about finding someone else – someone who wanted children as much as she did. But it was Eddie's child that she had given up. And it was Eddie's child that she still grieved. She felt that the only way she could reclaim what she had lost was to have Eddie's child someday.

Morgan didn't really mean to get pregnant again. In fact, she wasn't even sure that she *could* get pregnant because of complications from the abortion. She took five home pregnancy tests, just to be sure.

Eddie was furious when she told him the results. He knew how much she wanted a baby, and he believed that she had done it on purpose. Morgan was angry too. For the first time, she was angry at Eddie for taking no responsibility for anything and then blaming Morgan when he was unhappy with the outcome.

She told Eddie that she was going to have the baby no matter what. But Eddie was more determined than she had ever seen him before. He told her that she would have to leave "his" house if she did.

His ultimatum was a wake-up call for Morgan. She didn't expect him to be thrilled, and she knew that without a ring on her finger she didn't have a much security. But she never thought he would threaten to throw her out of the home that she had paid for – especially when she was pregnant.

Morgan didn't know where to turn. After her mother's response the last time, she didn't feel that she could confide in her. But she didn't want to stay another night with Eddie. She went to a friend's apartment for a few days, and then she called her mom.

This time, her mother was more supportive. Morgan and her mother hadn't talked much since the abortion. But her mother had almost as many regrets about it as Morgan herself. She had responded to Morgan's crisis with fear, but the situation had caused her to take a second look at her life. *She* had had an abortion when she was younger. When she told Morgan that getting pregnant had ruined her marriage, she wasn't talking about her pregnancy with Morgan. She and Morgan's father had gotten married because she was pregnant before that. However, he had resented their "shotgun" wedding, and they fought constantly. Morgan's mother decided to abort the baby because she didn't want to bring a child into all that conflict. She had gotten pregnant with Morgan, a year later. The arguments continued, however, all through her second, third and fourth pregnancies – until she and her husband finally divorced. Yet, Morgan's mother never stopped missing the child she had lost. She tried to fill the void in different ways. When Morgan had told her that she was pregnant, she was confronted by many painful memories that she had tried to suppress. She wanted to shut out the past and avoid the future, as well. But instead, she found herself living with the pain and emptiness of yet another loss.

Morgan was surprised by her mother's revelation. She felt sorry for her, but she was relieved to know that her mother understood her pain. They cried together over all that they had lost – and then, when they were through, they began to talk about their hopes for the future, as well.

Morgan really wanted to keep her baby, this time, even though she was afraid. Her anger in the face of Eddie's opposition had temporarily steeled her determination. But she still had many doubts. She worried that she wouldn't be a good mother and was frightened about her baby's future. The pregnancy had heightened Morgan's feelings of guilt over the abortion. She wondered how she could bond with the baby she was carrying when she was still grieving over the one she gave up.

Morgan's mother shared with her that she had gotten help by attending a *Rachel Network Evening of Prayer*. She offered to accompany Morgan to one of the services if she wanted to go. Morgan was willing to try anything. She knew that something had to change.

She invited Eddie to come with her too. She felt sure that he must have grief over their loss even though he never talked about it. However, Eddie denied needing any help, and he had no interest in going along to support Morgan. In fact, he didn't want *her* to go either. Going to church was not something Morgan had ever done before, and the idea of doing anything different scared him. He didn't want their relationship to change.

Eddie made excuses to keep Morgan from going. In spite of the fact that he had threatened to throw her out of the house, he claimed to need her at home on the night of the service. He said that he was sick. Morgan came by the house to make him dinner and promised to come home again that night, just to check on him. But she insisted that she had to go: *she was determined not to miss this chance to finally find some peace.*

As she sat down at the church, she realized that going to the Evening of Prayer was the first thing she had ever really done just for herself. It was also the first time she had ever said no to Eddie. She felt a little anxious knowing that he was at home feeling neglected, but she also felt a sense of peace believing that she had made the right choice this time.

Having her mother's support made a big difference. As they prayed for healing and reconciliation, Morgan was comforted by her mother's hand on hers. She felt closer to her than ever. She also felt close to God for the first time. She had never before felt His presence, but He felt very real to her that night.

The true moment of healing came, however, as Morgan closed her eyes and pictured her baby in the arms of the Lord. She wondered if she should really give him a name. She would have liked to have asked Eddie for his input but, of course, he wasn't there. And since he had wanted nothing to do with their baby when she was pregnant the first time, she could hardly expect him to bond with him now, after so much time had passed. Yet, in spite of that, she decided to name the baby after him. Little Eddie would always be his son – *no matter what* – and she felt that he was entitled to be named after his father.

Morgan left the church feeling a new sense of strength. She wasn't exactly sure about what had changed, but something felt very different. When her mother started to drive her home, Morgan abruptly asked her to turn around. She called Eddie and told him that she was going to spend the night with her mom. Eddie was furious – he told her to come home right away. She hung up the phone quickly to avoid giving in. The next day, her mother brought her back to the house to pick up her clothes while

Eddie was gone. Morgan didn't have much to take with her. She had nothing of her own but her hair dryer and a few clothes.

Her mother was happy to give Morgan her old room back. And Morgan was surprised at how comfortable she felt there. She didn't have many happy memories of her life in that house, but her focus wasn't on the past anymore. She was thinking about her future, instead, and her old room seemed like the perfect place for her to start her life over again.

She missed Eddie terribly. But after the *Rachel Network Evening of Prayer*, she no longer felt that she needed him to maintain a connection with the child they had lost. She knew that Little Eddie was with God, and that God was with her, and they were all *together* somehow in His love. She no longer felt that she would be losing a part of herself if she left Eddie.

Eddie called her constantly and begged her to come back. She told him she would think about it, but she was determined not to go anywhere until after her baby was born. She needed to take care of herself – and to be taken care of – as she awaited the arrival of her new son. Her mother was there for her in a way that no one ever had been before. As hard as it was for Morgan to be in the role of receiving help rather than giving it, she was determined to get whatever she needed to bring her pregnancy to a happy conclusion.

Day by day, Morgan learned more about herself and discovered her own strengths. By the time the baby was born, she felt excited about the challenges that lay ahead, and she believed that she had the ability to be a good mother. She named her son Gavin, after her grandfather, because he was the strongest man she had ever known. She wanted her son to grow up feeling the sense of strength that it had taken her so long to find.

Eddie, however, wasn't feeling so strong. Without Morgan, his life seemed to be falling apart. Morgan felt sorry for him, but she wasn't willing to live with Eddie on their old terms. Until Eddie was ready to be married and have a family, she decided to stay right where she was.

Eddie began to realize that he was going to have to start taking some responsibility if he wanted Morgan in his life. He got a regular job, so that he could pay his child support, and began going to church with Morgan on Sundays.

By reconnecting with herself, Morgan was able to become the mother that she had always wanted to be. And though she realizes that Eddie may never become the father that she wanted for her son, he is slowly learning to take responsibility for himself and for Gavin. Morgan had never been able to change Eddie by catering to his demands. But by demanding respect for herself, she motivated him to grow up. Now, she is determined to continue to grow in her relationship with her baby, with God and with herself.

Scripture for Meditation:

"I can do all things in God who strengthens me." (Philippians 4:13)

"Each of you has been given special gifts out of God's manifold grace. Use them to help each other, passing on to others the blessings you have received." (1 Peter 4:10)

"For I know well the plans I have in mind for you, plans for good and not for evil – plans to give you a future full of hope." (Jeremiah 29:11)

"Each of us has received God's favor in the measure that Christ bestows it." (Ephesians 4:7)

"…You are precious to me, and honored, and I love you." (Isaiah 43:4)
"For freedom Christ has set you free – so stand firm and do not take on the yoke of slavery a second time." (Galatians 5:1)

"May the God of our Lord Jesus Christ, the Father of glory, grant you a spirit of wisdom and insight to know Him clearly. May He enlighten your innermost vision that you may know the great hope to which He has called you, the wealth of His glorious heritage to be distributed among the members of the church, and the immeasurable scope of His power in us who believe. It is like the strength He showed in raising Christ from the dead and seating him at His right hand in Heaven high above every principality and power …." (Ephesians 1:17-21)

Prayer:

Lord, we thank You for the plans that You have for our lives, and for the gifts that You have given us. Thank You for the freedom You have granted us to fulfill our hopes and dreams. Enlighten us with the vision to understand ourselves and to know how we can live more fully in You.

When guilt and fear make us lose our sense of who we really are, let Your Spirit remind us of Your glory. Transform us into the men and women You created us to be. When the pressures of the world and the expectations of others threaten to make us lose our way, lead us back to the lives that You have designed for all eternity – lives of purpose and meaning, lives that have a hidden glory to be revealed only by You.

Amen.

Review of Practical Suggestions

1. Reading for Growth: It can be difficult to find reading material for post-abortion issues. There are sections in bookstores for almost every form of recovery, but abortion-related healing goes largely unmentioned. Nevertheless, there are some good materials available. *Forbidden Grief,* by Theresa Burke and David Reardon (2002) is one book that has broken the code of silence. Check out the Rachel Network Website at http://www.rachelnetwork.org for other suggestions and ideas. Look for books that promote personal growth and provide encouragement to live your life more fully. The lives of the Saints can be a great resource – especially biographies of saints who experienced brokenness before they found the transforming love of God. The Scriptures are filled with stories of ordinary men and women doing great things while struggling with their own human frailty. Learning from people who have overcome obstacles and discovered their mission in life can be encouraging to those who are attempting to find themselves and to realize their potential.

2. *The Letter:* Writing a letter to someone else can be freeing, but writing a letter to yourself can be powerful as well. A letter of *affirmation* is a great way to nurture your spirit. You can address this letter to yourself as an adult or as a child. For those who missed out on nurturing from parents, writing a letter to the *child within* can be especially healing. Whatever you most needed to hear as a child can be written down in a note or card to be read and re-read for encouragement.

3. *Rediscovering Hopes and Dreams:* One of the characteristics of post-traumatic stress (whether from an abortion or from other traumas) is a foreshortened or diminished sense of the future. After being traumatized, it can be hard to plan for your life ahead or to believe that dreams can come true. Try journaling and looking at old scrapbooks to reconnect with childhood dreams. Or start a new scrapbook to represent your future instead of your past. Pray for inspiration to discover *a vision* for your life. Regaining a sense of God's plans, reclaiming old hopes, and finding *new aspirations* are all a part of the restoration that God intends for your life.

Notes:

Notes:

Notes:

Notes:

Notes:

Notes:

Appendix for Priests:

Issues to Consider Regarding Health Concerns and the Sacrament of the Anointing of the Sick

Father John Hardon, S.J., in his 1975 book, *The Catholic Catechism*, said that the changes in the Sacrament of the Anointing of the Sick following Vatican II were "more far-reaching than for any other sacrament in the Catholic liturgy." In his opinion, the most significant changes were "those pertaining to the persons for whom the anointing is intended and the circumstances under which the rite is to be administered." The degree of change may explain why there seems to be some variability in how the sacrament is understood, today, by many Catholic adults. But before looking at what's changed, let's look at what hasn't changed ...

Effects of the sacrament. Hardon's book says that there are a "cluster" of effects, all stemming from the central "gift of the Holy Spirit." He cites the **Council of Trent** in identifying effects that include the following:

- "It alleviates and strengthens the soul of the sick person."

- "It gives him great confidence in the divine mercy."

- "The sick person more easily resists the temptations of the devil ...."

- "[It] … takes away sins, if there are any still to be expiated, and removes the traces of sin."

- "This anointing occasionally restores health to the body if health would be of advantage to the salvation of the soul."   (p. 542)

In his introduction to this sacrament, Hardon said its purpose is "to give spiritual aid and strength and perfect spiritual health, including, if need be the remission of sins. Conditionally it also restores bodily health …." (p. 540)

It is clear from this that the primary effects of the sacrament are spiritual. In thinking about the use of this sacrament with women and men who have experienced abortion, it is interesting to note the effect of giving "great confidence in the divine mercy." Many men and women who have been involved in abortion repeatedly confess the abortion to different priests, not able to believe that they have been forgiven. The grace of "confidence in the divine mercy" is important for anyone suffering with illness, but for post-abortive women suffering from recurrent guilt such assurance is of even greater value.

Another effect of the sacrament is being able to resist temptation. What kind of temptations would the dying patient have been subject to centuries ago during the time of the Council of Trent? If death were imminent, in a day when pain control was very limited, might there have been a temptation to suicide? That's one temptation that clearly affects post-abortive women today. Large, record-based studies have shown a higher rate of suicide after abortion. In fact, one 1996 study found that women who have had an abortion have a **650 percent higher risk of death from suicide** compared to women who carry their babies to term

(Gissler, Hemmink, and Lonnqvist). This temptation can persist for years. A study examining records for over 150,000 California women, again, showed an increased risk of suicide in post-abortive women for a period of up to eight years after their abortions (Reardon, Ney, Scheuren, Cougle, Coleman, Strahan, 2002). There are also reports of attempted or completed suicides coinciding with the anniversary date of the abortion or expected due date of the aborted child (Tischler, C. 1981).

Another serious temptation facing post-abortive women is the temptation to have *repeat* abortions. It is not uncommon to encounter participants on Rachel's Vineyard Retreats™ who have had multiple abortions. (We've personally known more than one woman who'd had twelve or more abortions, and two or three is common). It is important to understand that women are not simply "using abortion as birth control." Rather, they are dealing with extremely painful and conflicting emotions, in many cases. Women who have had one abortion often have a strong desire for another child to replace the one they've lost yet, once they conceive again, the pregnancy can serve as a reminder of painful issues from the earlier abortion. Unable to deal with the overwhelming emotions resulting from the new pregnancy, and perhaps facing circumstances that are still as difficult as before, the woman may be propelled into another and still another abortion. The book, *Forbidden Grief,* by Theresa Burke, Ph.D. and David Reardon, Ph.D. explains this process in more depth.

The same dynamics can operate when the daughter or granddaughter of a post-abortive woman becomes pregnant while unmarried. Because of severe anxiety over unresolved issues regarding their own abortion, it is not unusual for post-abortive women to become instrumental in

122

the abortions of the next generation, making the appointments and driving the younger women to the clinics and, in some cases, *insisting on the abortion.* Might the spiritual healing of the anointing and the accompanying *grace to resist temptation* help to prevent this cycle of abortion in the lives of individual women and in the next generation?

Who May be Anointed?

Certainly, during the period prior to Vatican II, the sacrament was reserved for people suffering from physical illness in which there was an *imminent* danger of death. Today, however, Canon Law speaks in terms of the time when one *begins* to be in danger of death, by old age or illness (Can. 1004).

Although Canon Law does require that the illness be serious, Canon 1005 says that, "This sacrament is to be administered when there is a doubt ... whether the person is dangerously ill." Father Hardon, in his catechism, quoting provisions issued by the Holy See, had this to say: "How may one judge the gravity of the illness that permits the conferring of this sacrament? 'It is sufficient, to have a prudent or probable judgment about its seriousness. All anxiety about the matter ought to be put aside and, if necessary, the physician might be consulted.'"

How Might this Apply to Post-abortive Women?

The abortion represents a major trauma to the woman's body. It is a serious, invasive surgical procedure. But it's hard to know the exact numbers and types of medical complications from abortion, even when the effects are serious and potentially fatal. There are several reasons for this. For one thing, there are no federal or state regulations requiring the reporting of abortion complications in the U.S. and, not surprisingly, most abortionists are not inclined to report voluntarily. Indeed, the abortionist often would not know about complications since women usually do not follow up with the abortionist for their routine medical care. Because of shame, women may not disclose the abortion to their regular physician, who would then be unable to link later problems to an abortion.

Despite these and other difficulties, the truth about the serious medical consequences of abortion is now being reported in mainstream, peer reviewed medical journals in the U.S., Canada, and western Europe. The recent book *Detrimental Affects of Abortion: An Annotated Bibliography* lists 1200 entries in 140 categories, with each entry including a citation to published studies. The print version of this reference book, published in 2001, does not include approximately sixty more recent studies which have been added to a supplement which is available by e-mail.

We've already touched on the drastically increased suicide rate after abortion, but there are increased deaths from a variety of other causes, over an extended period after the abortion. However, attempting to study deaths related to abortion is extremely challenging, since the international standard for medical coding specifies that if a woman dies from an abortion, the immediate cause of death (blood clot, bleeding to death, infection) is to be coded, rather than the abortion, as cause of death. In addition, rescarch is often affected by political agendas. Further, the International Classification of Diseases requires that to be counted as a "maternal death," the death must occur while the woman is pregnant or within 42 days of the birth or the abortion.

But one can easily see that a suicide on the one-year anniversary of an abortion would not fall within the 42-day period. Additionally, "incidental" deaths that were not thought to be related to the pregnancy would not be "counted," so deaths from cancer, heart attacks, suicide or other causes not expected to be related to the abortion would be missed.

Most women would not have a clear understanding of the full physical effects of abortion because of lack of informed consent in the abortion industry. One woman commented: "I was given more information before my dog had surgery, than when I had my abortion." While it is important not to frighten women after the fact with statistics that were not available to them before the procedure, there *are* a number of studies that demonstrate a higher death rate among post-abortive women. Setting aside for a moment the increased rates of death by suicide, as well as an increased rate of deaths by accident, a recent review of medical literature has found research showing that women who had an abortion have been found to have a 60 percent higher risk of death from natural causes compared to women who gave birth. There are many possible reasons for this, but it is known that depression is associated with suppression of the immune system, which could increase the risk of infections and cancers (Reardon, Strahan, Thorp, Shuping, 2004).

This review article also found that women are three times more likely to die of heart disease during the eight years after an abortion, and over five times more likely to die of stroke after abortion compared to women who delivered.

Other serious consequences of abortion are currently being studied. However, women are already beginning to take legal action against the industry for withholding information regarding health risks. Unfortunately as these health risks become more known and publicized, some women express that this knowledge frightens them, and makes them feel they are being punished by God. Women who have accepted God's forgiveness and returned to the sacraments have reported feeling alienated from God all over again when they contemplate the possibility of an early death from a potentially fatal, abortion-related illness.

The Sacrament of the Anointing of the Sick would seem to be particularly helpful for women in this situation, to help them to more deeply connect with the mercy of God. No one (whether they are preparing for gall bladder surgery or recovering from an abortion) wants to hear that they are "beginning to be in danger of death." Nevertheless, for those who are recuperating from a variety of conditions or undergoing various types of medical treatment and procedures including abortion, this sacrament might be offered with an emphasis on the hope for healing.

It is likely that most post-abortive men and women would *not* request the anointing, for numerous reasons – from lack of catechesis about the sacrament, to guilt and shame about the abortion and its effects. Because of this, many who might benefit from the sacrament never receive it. Priests should to be especially alert to instances where the anointing would be appropriate to offer to post-abortive individuals who might welcome it as an opportunity to receive God's grace and healing.

126

Notes:

Notes:

Notes:

Notes:

References

Burke, T.K., Burke, K. (1999). *Rachel's Vineyard Retreat™ weekend retreat manual.* King of Prussia, PA: Rachel's Vineyard Retreat ™

Burke, T.K., Reardon, D. (2002). *Forbidden grief.* Springfield, IL: Acorn Books.

Canon Law Society, translator. (1983, 1995). *Code of Canon Law, Latin English Edition.* Washington, D.C.: Canon Law Society of America.

Council of Trent, *Doctrine on the Sacrament of Extreme Unction,* I: Denzinger 909 (1696).

Gissler, M., Hemminki, E. Lonnqvist, J (1996). *Suicides after pregnancy in Finland: 1987-1994.* British Medical Journal 313:1431-1434

Hardon, J. (1975). *The Catholic Catechism.* Garden City, NY: Doubleday and Company, Inc.

Hayford, J. (1986, 1990). *I'll hold you in Heaven.* Ventura, CA: Regal Books.

John Paul II (1995). *Evangelium vitae (the Gospel of life).* Origins CNS Documentary Service Vol. 24: No. 42 Paragraph 99.

Irwin, M., Daniels, M., Bloom, E., Smith.T., Weiner, H. (1987). *Life events, depressive symptoms and immune function.* American Journal of Psychiatry 144:437-41.

Linkins, R, Comstock, G. (1990). *Depressed mood and development of cancer.* 132 (5): 962

McAll, K., Wilson, W. (1987) *Grief after abortion.* Southern Medical Journal. 80 (7): 817-821.

McDaniel, D. (2002, 2007). *In the garden of the new creation: a rebirth of the self in the spirit.* Winston-Salem, NC: Tabor Garden Press

Reardon, D. (1987). *Aborted women, silent no more.* Chicago: Loyola University Press

Reardon, D. Ney, P., Scheuren, F. Cougle, J. Coleman, P. Strahan T. (2002). *Deaths associated with pregnancy outcome: a record linkage study of low income women,* Southern Medical Journal, 95 (8): 834-841.

Reardon, D., Strahan, Jr. J., Thorp, J. Shuping, M. (2004). *Deaths associated with abortion compared to childbirth – a review of new and old data and the medical and legal implications.* The Journal of Contemporary Health Law & Policy.

Reardon, D. (1996) *The Jericho Plan: Breaking Down the Walls Which Prevent Post-Abortion Healing.* Springfield, Illinois, Acorn Books

Shuping, M.W. (2004). *Rachel Network evening of prayer for healing after abortion.* Winston-Salem, North Carolina, Rachel Network

Tischler, C. (1981). *Adolescent suicide attempts following elective abortion.* Pediatrics 68(5): 670-671

United States Catholic Conference (1983). *Pastoral Care of the Sick: introduction and pastoral notes.* The English Translation of the "Introduction" and "Pastoral Notes" from *Pastoral Care of the Sick: Rites of Anointing and Viaticum, 1982,* Washington, D.C.: International Committee on English in the Liturgy, Inc.

World Health Organization (1978), *International statistical classification of diseases and related health problems, 9th revision.* Vol. 1. Geneva: World Health Organization.

Books and Materials by Martha Shuping, M.D.

The Four Steps to Healing,
Martha Shuping, M.D. and Debbie McDaniel, M.A. LPC

Rachel Network Evening of Prayer for Healing After Abortion: Leaders Guide, by Martha Shuping, M.D. (Includes all the prayers for this service and background information for leaders.)

Rachel Network Evening of Prayer for Healing After Abortion: Videotape, *M. Shuping.* (Contains a demonstration of the service to be used for leaders' training or for individual prayer and reflection.)

For information contact:

rachel@rachelnetwork.org
or visit
http://www.rachelnetwork.org

Other Books by
Debbie McDaniel, M.A. LPC

In the Garden of the New Creation:
A Rebirth of the Self in the Spirit
Tabor Garden Press

Let Your Light Shine:
Living Reflections on the Light of the Word
Tabor Garden Press

For information about available titles or trainings contact:
books@taborgardenpress.com

Or see our website at:
http://www.taborgardenpress.com